Methamphetamine

DRUGS The Straight Facts

Alcohol
Alzheimer's and Memory Drugs
Anti-anxiety Drugs
Antidepressants
Barbiturates
Birth Control Pills
Body Enhancement Products
Cancer Drugs
Cocaine
Codeine
Date Rape Drugs
Designer Drugs
Diet Pills
Ecstasy
Hallucinogens
Heroin
HIV/AIDS Treatment Drugs
Inhalants
Marijuana
Morphine
Nicotine
Opium
Peyote and Mescaline
Prescription Pain Relievers
Ritalin and Other Methylphenidate-Containing Drugs
Sleep Aids

■ DRUGS
The Straight Facts

Methamphetamine

Randi Mehling

Consulting Editor
David J. Triggle
University Professor
School of Pharmacy and Pharmaceutical Sciences
State University of New York at Buffalo

CHELSEA HOUSE
PUBLISHERS
An imprint of Infobase Publishing

Drugs The Straight Facts: Methamphetamine

Chelsea House
An imprint of Infobase Publishing
132 West 31st Street
New York, NY 10001

Library of Congress Cataloging-in-Publication Data
Mehling, Randi.
  Methamphetamine / Randi Mehling.
    p. cm. — (Drugs. The straight facts)
  Includes bibliographical references and index.
  ISBN-13: 978-0-7910-9532-4
  ISBN-10: 0-7910-9532-0
  1. Methamphetamine—Juvenile literature. 2. Methamphetamine abuse—
Juvenile literature. I. Title. II. Series.
  RC568.A45M43 2007
  616.86'4—dc22

                                                      2007019629

Chelsea House books are available at special discounts when purchased in bulk quantities for businesses, associations, institutions, or sales promotions. Please call our Special Sales Department in New York at (212) 967-8800 or (800) 322-8755.

You can find Chelsea House on the World Wide Web at
http://www.chelseahouse.com

Text design by Terry Mallon

Cover design by Keith Trego

Illustrations by Melissa Erickson

Printed in the United States of America

Bang EJB 10 9 8 7 6 5 4 3 2 1

This book is printed on acid-free paper.

All links and Web addresses were checked and verified to be correct at the time of publication. Because of the dynamic nature of the Web, some addresses and links may have changed since publication and may no longer be valid.

Table of Contents

The Use and Abuse of Drugs

The issues associated with drug use and abuse in contemporary society are vexing subjects, fraught with political agendas and ideals that often obscure essential information that teens need to know to have intelligent discussions about how to best deal with the problems associated with drug use and abuse. *Drugs: The Straight Facts* aims to provide this essential information through straightforward explanations of how an individual drug or group of drugs works in both therapeutic and non-therapeutic conditions; with historical information about the use and abuse of specific drugs with discussion of drug policies in the United States; and with an ample list of further reading.

From the start, the series uses the word *drug* to describe psychoactive substances that are used for medicinal or non-medicinal purposes. Included in this broad category are substances that are legal or illegal. It is worth noting that humans have used many of these substances for hundreds, if not thousands of years. For example, traces of marijuana and cocaine have been found in Egyptian mummies; the use of peyote and Amanita fungi has long been a component of religious ceremonies worldwide; and alcohol production and consumption have been an integral part of many human cultures' social and religious ceremonies. One can speculate about why early human societies used such drugs, but very likely it was for the same reasons we do—namely, to relieve pain and to heal wounds. Perhaps anything that could give people a break from the poor conditions and the fatigue associated with hard work was considered a welcome tonic. Life in premodern cultures was likely to be, in the memorable words of 17th-century English philosopher Thomas Hobbes, "poor, nasty, brutish, and short." One can also speculate about modern human societies' continued use and abuse of drugs. Whatever the reasons, the consequences of sustained drug use are not insignificant—addiction, unwanted side effects, overdose, and, for illegal, nonprescription drugs, incarceration, and drug wars—and must be dealt with by an informed citizenry.

The problem that faces our society today is how to break the connection between our demand for drugs and the willingness of largely outside countries to supply this highly profitable trade. This is the same problem we have faced since narcotics and cocaine were outlawed by the Harrison Narcotic Act of 1914, and we have yet to defeat it despite current expenditures in excess of approximately $20 billion per year on "the war on drugs" and the incarceration of a significant fraction of our citizens, particularly of minorities. The first step in meeting any challenge is to become informed about the nature of the challenge. The purpose of this series is to educate our readers so that they can make informed decisions about issues related to drugs and drug abuse.

SUGGESTED ADDITIONAL READING

Courtwright, David T. *Forces of Habit, Drugs and the Making of the Modern World.* Cambridge, Mass.: Harvard University Press, 2001. David T. Courtwright is professor of history at the University of North Florida.

Davenport-Hines, Richard. *The Pursuit of Oblivion: A Global History of Narcotics.* New York: Norton, 2002. The author is a professional historian and a member of the Royal Historical Society.

Huxley, Aldous. *Brave New World.* New York: Harper & Row, 1932. Huxley's book, written in 1932, paints a picture of a cloned society devoted only to the pursuit of happiness.

David J. Triggle, Ph.D.
University Professor
School of Pharmacy and Pharmaceutical Sciences
State University of New York at Buffalo

Introduction

Ice. Crystal. Tweakers. Raves. Narcolepsy. Dope. Amped. Psychosis. Alert. Smurfing. Dopamine. Jittery. Sudafed. Meth labs. Explosions. Paranoia. Crashing. Obesity. Railing. Brain Cravings. Euphoria. Depression.

What do all of these words have in common? Methamphetamine, or simply meth. Yet there is nothing simple about this stimulating and highly addictive drug. Meth speeds up the nervous system. It makes you feel alert, focused, and euphoric, with powerful feelings of pleasure—at first. Then meth slams you to the ground as intensely as it lifts you up, with crushing depression, fatigue, and the inability to feel any pleasure. The brain develops tolerance to meth almost immediately, and starts to crave it. Meth creates dependency, and it is one of the hardest drugs to quit.

Over the past 10 years, meth use has increased dramatically in the United States. The number of people over the age of 12 who have tried meth at least once in their lifetime was 1.8 million in 1994. Just three years later, this number tripled to 5.3 million. By 1999, lifetime use had nearly doubled again to 9.4 million. Today, it is estimated that over 12 million people have used meth at least once. Teen meth use has actually declined slightly over this time, yet many teenagers suffer from meth dependency and addiction.

Meth is illegal to use, possess, manufacture, or distribute, except with a prescription from a doctor. These prescriptions are very limited and closely monitored because of meth's high potential for addiction. The federal penalty for a first offense is a five- to 40-year prison term, along with a fine of up to $2 million, depending on the amount of meth and other circumstances. If using, possessing, manufacturing, or distributing meth near a child, new laws have made penalties even stronger.

These and other statistics, such as the increasing number of meth labs and the growing number of Americans requiring treatment for meth abuse, contribute to the numerous media headlines telling us there is a meth epidemic in our country.

Why do teenagers use meth? How many teens actually use it? How does meth affect the brain? How can you tell if your friend is using meth? What are meth labs, and how do they affect teenagers and the community? Is there a meth epidemic?

Scientific research from many sources has been collected and presented in this book to address these questions. The purpose of this book is to help teenagers understand all aspects of meth use—its psychological, social, legal, community, and health consequences—so teens can decide for themselves what this drug is really all about.

1

The History of Methamphetamine

The first time I tried meth, I was 13. I didn't do it again, though, until I was 15. I used meth only sporadically until I was 17, when I started using and selling it regularly. I sold for about two years. My friend and I mostly sold to support our own habit. We sold balls of crank that could keep you up for a week.

I wasn't in school because I'd been kicked out at 14 on suspicion of taking drugs. Any money I earned went down the drain. I'd sell an ounce, then I'd do a half ounce in a few days. I lost touch with reality. Once I was up for seven days. I was at a friend's house and thought I saw a guy shoot someone. I started to destroy the house until I realized the whole vision was what's called a night terror.

I finally realized I needed help when this girl and I were in the car. It was pouring, and I was driving 85 miles an hour. The car was hydro-planing, and the girl was crying because she thought we were going to die. When we got to our destination, I thought, "This is someone I care about. This is what I do to people." I was so sick of myself. Three weeks later, I checked into rehab.

I've been clean for almost three years. When I look back on my life as an addict, it's like someone else's life. I missed out on so much: meeting girls in high school, playing football. But I got my GED, and now I have a good job in construction. If I could tell kids anything, it's that you have no control over how drugs will affect you. It's an evil cycle, and the only way to stop the cycle is never to start it.

—Z.B., 22, Seattle, Washington[1]

THE BIRTH OF METHAMPHETAMINE

Methamphetamine is a **stimulant** drug, similar to cocaine, which is derived from the coca plant, but made entirely of human-made chemicals (**synthetic**). Some stimulants are used every day by many people; others, like amphetamines, are available only with a doctor's prescription; and some, like cocaine, have no legal use whatsoever. One everyday stimulant is caffeine, which exists naturally in coffee, chocolate, and many sodas. Whether natural or chemical, legal or illegal, stimulants speed up the nervous system. Stimulants in regular doses can make some people feel awake, alert, energetic, and not hungry. Too much stimulant can create unpleasant skin-crawling, jittery sensations for some, but euphoria for others.

Methamphetamine is more powerful than cocaine or any natural stimulant. When taken in large amounts, it can cause violence, hallucinations, and **psychosis**. Typically methamphetamine is produced as a crystal-like powder, a larger chunk of crystal, or in tablets. It can be snorted, eaten, smoked, or injected. It has dozens of street names but is most often called *meth*. It is also known as *crank*, *glass*, *speed*, and *ice*. Motorcycle gangs in the 1970s used to hide meth in the crank cases of their bikes, leading to the nickname *crank*. The terms *ice* or *glass* come from the rock-like form of meth, which, in contrast to its powdered form, looks like pieces of ice or glass.[2, 3, 4]

Although methamphetamine is synthetic, it traces its roots to a small leafless bush called *Ephedra* that grows in China and North America. For more than 5,000 years, Chinese healers have dried and boiled the stems of this plant to make a tea called *mahuang* that opens air passages and makes breathing easier, helping those suffering from asthma and other respiratory illnesses. The tea also increases energy and general well being. In 1847, when Mormons settled in Utah, they discovered that the native peoples of the western United States enjoyed an exciting drink made from *Ephedra*. Since

Figure 1.1 The ephedra sinica bush is used to make mahuang and ephedrine, stimulants used to fight colds and asthma, but it is also one of the ingredients in amphetamines and methamphetamines. © Dagmar Ehling/Photo Researchers, Inc.

coffee and tea were forbidden by their religion, the Mormons named it "Mormon tea," and enjoyed frequent cups of this stimulating brew.[2]

In the late 1800s, scientists isolated ephedrine (named after its biological name *Ephedra*) as the active compound in *mahuang*. In 1887, a German chemist succeeded in creating the synthetic drug amphetamine that had the same stimulating effects as ephedrine. Lacking any identifiable medical use, the drug was shelved.[5]

In 1919, a Japanese chemist synthesized methamphetamine. It was easier to make than amphetamine and produced a crystalline powder that could be injected **intravenously** (directly into the veins), snorted, or mixed in a beverage. Methamphetamine was found to be very potent, with greater and longer lasting stimulating effects than amphetamine, especially when injected.[5]

Eli Lilly, a pharmaceutical company, manufactured a new asthma drug using ephedrine in the 1920s. At the time, ephedrine had to be **extracted** from limited supplies of the *Ephedra* plant; no one had figured out yet how to make a synthetic version of ephedrine from laboratory chemicals alone. However, in 1927, an American researcher named Gordon Alles recognized the therapeutic potential of amphetamines and realized that amphetamine could be used as a chemical substitute for the plant version of ephedrine. Beginning in 1932, amphetamine was marketed as an easily available nasal inhaler called Benzedrine. This new drug provided relief from nasal congestion for asthmatics and people with allergies and colds. In 1937, a tablet form of amphetamine became available by prescription to treat **narcolepsy** (a sleeping disorder), obesity, and attention deficit hyperactivity disorder (ADHD).[5, 6]

Throughout human history, people have sought to escape reality with mind-altering substances. Amphetamines proved no exception. People discovered that amphetamines increased energy and sexual **libido** while decreasing appetite and the need for sleep. In higher amounts, they also produced a euphoric high. In the 1950s and 1960s, doctors prescribed the drug frequently, and the use and eventual abuse of amphetamines soared during this time.[5]

METH SOLDIERS ON

During World War II, nearly every army was fueled by high quantities of amphetamine pills. Amphetamines curbed German, English, Japanese, and American soldiers' appetites in the face of limited food rations. The drug helped soldiers fight

PRONUNCIATION GUIDE

methamphetamine (meth-am-FET-a-meen)

ephedrine (eh-FEH-drin)

psuedoephedrine (sue-dough-eh-FEH-drin)

Table 1.1 Effects of Meth Use

Short-term effects of meth use can include:[7]	Long-term effects of meth use can include:[7]
• increased attention	• dependence and addiction
• increased activity	• paranoia
• decreased fatigue	• hallucinations and psychosis
• decreased appetite	• mood disturbances
• euphoria and rush	• repetitive motor activity
• increased respiration	• stroke
• hyperthermia	• weight loss

fatigue, keeping them alert at their posts without need for sleep. At his doctor's request, Winston Churchill took amphetamines to stay awake, and American troops received amphetamine as well as methamphetamine pills along with their food rations.[2]

Under Hitler's command, German chemists created and generously distributed a methamphetamine tablet called Pervitin to German troops. By the 1940s, the effects of large and frequent amounts of amphetamines and methamphetamine were well documented. These effects included aggressive, violent, and paranoid behavior as well as a tendency to lose the very basic human emotions of sympathy and compassion. It is reported that Hitler injected himself with methamphetamine as often as eight times a day; some historians speculate that he gave meth to his troops to create "killing machines" divorced from human empathy, and that he himself was addicted to the drug.[2, 5]

During the war, Japanese pilots on kamikaze (suicide) missions reportedly took methamphetamine before their fateful flights. After World War II, the Japanese public gained access to the military's stockpiled meth, creating hundreds of thousands of intravenous meth addicts there. Many soldiers returned to their homelands addicted to these stimulants, afflicted with methamphetamine/amphetamine psychosis. The Japanese banned the drug soon after World War II.[2, 5]

LEGALIZED METH AND SPEED FREAKS

By the 1950s and 1960s, meth was legally produced and sold over the counter as Methedrine and marketed to housewives as antidotes to depression and weight gain, to truckers to help them drive longer hauls without sleep, and to students and athletes seeking to push themselves longer and harder with greater energy and stamina. Today, methamphetamine is legally produced—yet rarely prescribed—in the United States as the drug Desoxyn to treat ADHD (attention deficit hyperactivity disorder), obesity, and narcolepsy.[9]

The widespread use of legal amphetamines and methamphetamine created many abusers, who were known as "speed freaks." They stayed up for days on end, lost significant amounts of weight due to lack of appetite, and eventually crashed into stupors. They often became jumpy, paranoid, and psychotic. After laws such as the 1970 federal Controlled Substances Act were passed to limit the availability of amphetamines, speed freaks, looking for a bigger high, began to shoot up (inject) methamphetamine, which was still legal and readily available. Soon the drug culture realized the dangers of shooting meth, and public health clinics, doctors, and even former

NAMES FOR METH

Batu Kilat (Malaysian term meaning shining rocks), Chalk, Crank, Crystallight, Devils Dandruff, Dope, Dummy Dust, Glass, Go-Go Juice, Haiwaiian Salt, High Speed Chicken Feed, Hillbilly Crack, Ice, Jenny Crank Program, Kryptonite, Methanfelony, Nazi Dope, Poop'd Out, Quartz, Rachet Jaw, Redneck Heroin, Rock, Rocket Fuel, Shabu, Shards, Stove Top, Smurf Dope, Sparkle, Tina, Vidrio (Spanish for glass)[3, 8] addicts promoted the slogan "Speed Kills" to warn others about it.[2, 10]

BIKER GANGS, MEXICAN DRUG CARTELS, AND SUPPLY AND DEMAND

In 1970, the federal government passed the Controlled Substances Act. This measure outlawed the use of injectable methamphetamine and sought to stem the use and abuse of meth by cutting off its supply. However, the market for meth did not disappear, and, as is the case with most drugs of abuse once they are made illegal, the supply was simply driven underground. (This is similar to what happened during Prohibition in the 1920s and early 1930s when the government outlawed the sale and consumption of alcohol. The result was a booming illegal alcohol industry run by powerful mob figures that supplied the millions who continued to drink.)

In the period immediately following the adoption of the Controlled Substances Act, the use of meth decreased. However, illicit (illegal) methamphetamine soon became available on the streets. During the 1970s, meth use was primarily associated with outlaw motorcycle gangs in California. To fill the growing demand for meth, a new, illegal, **clandestine** industry grew—the meth lab—as the bikers both used and manufactured meth.[2, 5, 10]

In the 1980s, highly organized cartels (organizations that control an entire industry) in Mexico took over the majority of meth manufacture, noting the business opportunity. They built giant warehouse "superlabs" that produced thousands of pounds of meth. These large drug "corporations" set up superlabs in Arizona and California, in addition to Mexico. The recreational use of methamphetamine skyrocketed.[11]

In the mid-1980s a new smokable form of meth, crystal meth (ice) was introduced to the growing meth market. Created in Asia, this "super-meth" was a much more potent version of meth, and its use quickly spread to Hawaii, and then to the Western states.[2]

Figure 1.2 A police officer views machinery at an ecstasy and methamphetamine factory near Serang, Indonesia. © M. Tohir/AP Images

In the late 1980s, these Mexican drug traffickers moved the majority of their meth business to California's Central Valley, setting up superlabs in the deserts and farm labor communities. Meth proved to be a very profitable business, and the December 2, 1989, edition of *The Economist* noted San Diego, California, had become the "methamphetamine capital of North America."[11]

These Mexican drug cartels are sophisticated and highly armed organizations; members do not usually take meth— they only sell it. Today, about 65 percent of all meth sold in the United States either is made in Mexico or produced in the United States by Mexican national drug traffickers in superlabs. They use skilled chemists to produce the drug, primarily in its purest form—crystal meth (ice).[10, 12]

MOM AND POP METH LABS

In the mid-1990s, American meth users realized they could make their own, less pure form of meth from recipes found on the Internet or in underground publications. Meth is easy to produce because all of the necessary ingredients are legal and have legitimate uses. Where the superlabs can make 80 or 100 pounds of meth during one "cook" cycle, these small-scale meth "cooks" produce less than a few ounces of meth at a time.[11] Small-scale mom and pop cooks usually intend to use the meth they make. They may also sell some to their friends or teach their friends how to manufacture the drug themselves. These home meth labs can fit into a suitcase, the trunk of a car, or a bathtub.

Athough meth is very easy to make, it is very danger-ous because the combination of necessary solvents and other chemicals is extraordinarily **flammable** and **volatile**. Many people have died or been seriously burned in meth lab explo-sions, and homes where meth is made require hazardous waste teams to clean up the toxic chemicals used to make meth before anyone can safely enter them again. Making meth in motel rooms has become popular. This is quite alarming, since in addition to the danger of an explosion that could set the entire motel on fire, the next guest in that same motel room will be exposed unknowingly to hazardous chemicals that lin-ger in the carpet, curtains, bed linens, etc.[11, 14]

THE METH EPIDEMIC

By 2005, law enforcement officials had discovered clandestine meth labs in every state (over 2,000 labs were found in Missouri

TERMS THAT DESCRIBE FEELING METH'S EFFECTS

Ampin', Cranked Up, Foiled, Gassing, Geeked, Gurped, Jacked, Ring Dang Doo, Spin-Jo Speeding, Spun Monkey or Spun Turkey, Twacked, Tweaked, Wired, Zoomin[3, 13]

Figure 1.3 A member of the Jasper County Drug Task Force in Joplin, Missouri, examines articles from a portable methamphetamine laboratory. © Mike Gullett/AP Images

alone in that year).[15] Since the 1990s, methamphetamine use has spread from the Western states to the Southwest and now appears to be concentrated in the rural Midwest. The drug's popularity is related to its low cost (as compared to other drugs), its availability, and its perceived pleasurable side effects such as euphoria, weight loss, and sexual enhancement. Internationally, meth, like the drug Ecstasy, has become a club drug of choice, popular with young people attending nightclubs and rave parties, particularly throughout Asia, but in the United States as well.[11, 16]

The intense, long-lasting highs of meth are accompanied by equally intense, long-lasting lows once the drug wears off. Because of the duration of the meth high, which lasts from six to over 14 hours, methamphetamine can create tolerance in the brain within *one* use.[7] This makes meth an extremely addictive drug. Meth damages brain cells related to memory, motor skills, and other vital bodily functions. The harmful effects on brain function in meth users seem to be only slowly reversible and may be irreversible.[17]

Over the years, meth users have morphed from rogue biker gang members and ravers, to housewives and the boy or girl next door who rely on the stimulation of meth to become superthin, superathletic, superstudents, or supermoms. Many rural teens report that they tried meth because they were bored. Based on the ever-increasing number of admissions

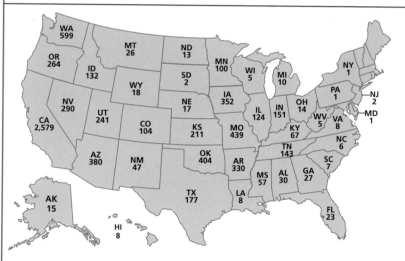

Total of All Meth Clandestine Laboratory Incidents Including Labs, Dumpsites, Chem/Glass/Equipment Calendar Year 1999

Source: National Clandestine Laboratory Database
Total: 7,438 / 43 states reporting
Dates: 01/01/99 to 12/31/99
© Infobase Publishing

Figure 1.4 The total number of methamphetamine laboratory incidents rose sharply from 1999 to 2003. It declined again by 2005, but these maps demonstrate the general spread of meth labs through the United States.

Calendar Year 2003

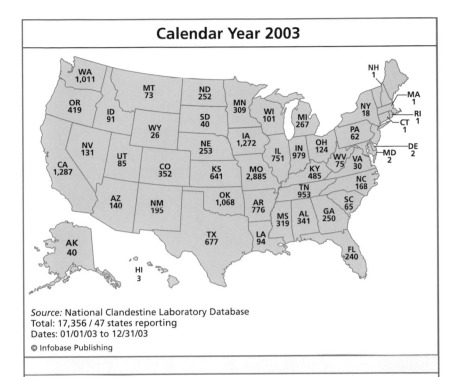

Source: National Clandestine Laboratory Database
Total: 17,356 / 47 states reporting
Dates: 01/01/03 to 12/31/03
© Infobase Publishing

Calendar Year 2005

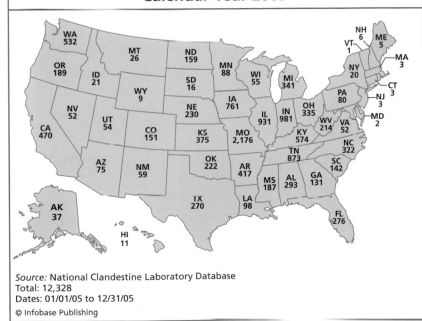

Source: National Clandestine Laboratory Database
Total: 12,328
Dates: 01/01/05 to 12/31/05
© Infobase Publishing

Figure 1.5 A member of the Southwest Virginia Clandestine Lab Team gathers ingredients and equipment used to make methamphetamine on the front lawn of a house that served as a secret methamphetamine laboratory. © Rain Smith/AP Images

of meth users to drug abuse treatment centers across the country,[18] as well as the increasing number of meth lab seizures, there is a widespread view that the United States is now in the midst of a meth epidemic. However, meth use and abuse is not a new problem. The United States has seen three

BEFORE WE BEGIN . . . A NOTE ON CRITICAL THINKING

When researching any topic, it is very important that you determine your source's credibility instead of taking what is said as accurate and truthful just because it is written in a book, a newspaper, or on the Internet. It is easy for people to present themselves as "experts" and produce "scientific evidence" to support their point of view. Ask yourself some questions about the validity of what you are reading, such as:

- Who is hosting the Internet site or who has written the book or article? What qualifications does the author have that convince you he or she is an expert in the field? Is the newspaper, journal, or Internet host presenting only one view, or is their reporting of the subject objective and unbiased?

- What is the date of the book, article, or posting? Is this relevant to your research or too outdated?

- If it is a scientific study, who funded or conducted the study? Is It peer-reviewed (judged by outside, independent experts)? Who published the book? Who is sponsoring the Web site? Would they have a bias or agenda in achieving a particular outcome?

- Was the actual number of subjects studied adequate to justify the results, or might chance have also played a role in arriving at the findings?

No single source of information can tell the whole story. Remember that this book is only one piece of a bigger puzzle in your quest for reliable information. Multiple sources from different areas are necessary to draw the fairest and most objective conclusion in your research paper. Explore, think critically, and decide for yourself!

waves of widespread meth use in its history: in the 1940s, 1950s, and 1960s, and again in the 1980s and 1990s. The claim of a meth "epidemic" therefore bears closer examination, especially when federal government surveys indicate teen meth use, contrary to public perception, actually has declined in recent years.[19] This book invites you to explore all of the evidence, learn about the effects of meth on the mind and body, its use, and its social and legal consequences so that you can reach your own conclusions.[5, 6, 10, 16]

2

The Hazards of Making Methamphetamine

Paul smoked pot with his friends and some older kids after school. One day, Gerry came around with a big smile on his face and asked, "Are you gonna tweak with us?" Paul wanted to be cool, and said, "Yeah," even though he wasn't sure what Gerry meant. "You have to keep your hands busy when you're tweaking, or you'll start picking at your face," warned Gerry, as he unwrapped a glass pipe from a piece of raggedy cloth. Gerry put what looked like a chunk of ice in the glass pipe. Paul watched nervously, silent. They sucked in its gray vapors after lighting it. Paul felt invincible and alive. He and his buddies were up for five days, and then he slept through an entire weekend. When he awoke, he felt hopeless and paranoid. He went to Gerry's house. It was filthy, and smelled like cat urine. When Gerry opened the door, Paul noticed his new friend looked like his house smelled. "Yo, dude, back for more?" Gerry didn't smile when he spoke. Paul slowly looked up from the ground to stare lethargically at Gerry. With great effort, he wordlessly turned around and walked back home.

Methamphetamine is a chemical that belongs to a class of drugs called stimulants that speed up the natural processes of the nervous system. Amphetamine is the chemical parent of methamphetamine. Although amphetamines are used as a substitute for ephedrine, the key ingredient for making meth is actually ephedrine or pseudoephedrine. [7]

EPHEDRINE AND PSEUDOEPHEDRINE

The chemicals ephedrine and pseudoephedrine are like cousins to each other. They share the same molecular formula but are structurally different. However, the structural differences between ephedrine and pseudoephedrine do not affect meth production since they are mirror images of each other. They can be used interchangeably as **precursors** in meth recipes. Precursors are substances that, in nature, might be inactive, but when combined with another chemical, create a new product. Methamphetamine starts with an inactive compound (ephedrine or pseudoephedrine) and other chemicals are added to produce the drug.[9, 11]

Ephedrine and pseudoephedrine are often used legally to alleviate congestion. When irritated, the tissues lining the inside of the nose and the respiratory system become swelled, which causes congestion. Ephedrine and pseudoephedrine cause the blood vessels to shrink, which brings down the swelling and allows easier breathing. Pseudoephedrine is used primarily in cold and allergy medications. Ephedrine is used more often in asthma medications as a **bronchodilator**. By acting on the blood vessels in the lungs, ephedrine helps ease breathing by relaxing and widening air passages.[7]

Only nine factories in the world make these two critical components of meth. There is one factory in Germany, one in the Czech Republic, two in China, and five in India. Super-labs run by illegal drug traffickers require large amounts of ephedrine or pseudoephedrine, and must purchase their supply of these chemicals from these international sources. Drug traffickers use sophisticated methods of acquiring these raw materials used to make meth including purchase through black market sources and obtaining the drugs from legal pharmaceutical warehouses. Cutting off this supply source would vastly reduce the street supply of methamphetamine.

Figure 2.1 In the Philippines workers stand guard over rows of metal drums containing ephedrine. © Pat Roque/AP Images

While U.S. drug enforcement recognizes this reality, international economic and political realities have made it difficult to accomplish this goal.[11]

THE MAKING OF METH

Meth is made using ordinary household utensils and appliances. Items such as coffee makers, blenders, microwaves, and mason jars are used in the cooking process. Seemingly ordinary, everyday products, such as matchbooks, camera batteries, rubbing alcohol, drain cleaner, engine starter fluid, brake cleaner, and table salt can be used in meth production. Because of the availability of these ingredients, a person can cook meth anywhere—the back of a pickup truck on the side of a highway, a recreational vehicle (RV) in a state park, and the house next door to an elementary school.[2, 20, 21]

Every stage of meth production is extremely hazardous because the solvents used (including alcohol, gasoline, acetone, and toluene) are extremely volatile and flammable. The slightest spark can *and does* easily ignite these solvents. Lithium obtained from camera batteries is often used in meth production. Lithium is a metal that reacts violently with water, creating heat and explosive hydrogen gas. Lithium can even ignite from the moisture in the air. This type of ignition could detonate the fumes from solvents used in the previous cooking phase. It is easy to understand how a meth cook with no training in chemistry can make fatal mistakes while cooking meth. Many mom and pop meth labs have exploded in flames, killing or injuring both the cook and innocents living in and around the lab. In addition, most of the solvents are also **carcinogens** (cancer-causing agents).[20, 21]

Phosphine gas may be produced as a by-product of the meth production process. Because of these highly flammable and **toxic** gases both *used* in meth production and *created* as a by-product of it, meth labs are considered hazardous waste zones in addition to being dangerously explosive.

METH AND THE COMMON COLD

In a 2005 study, scientists performed tests on a wide variety of over-the-counter cold medications found in pills, capsules, liquids, and liquid gels. They showed that any form of cold medicine containing pseudoephedrine can be used to manufacture methamphetamine. An average of 250 tablets and/or caplets was sufficient to produce one batch of meth. This is the standard amount of pseudoephedrine used by small-scale, illegal meth labs.[22]

SPEEDBALLS AND BIKER'S COFFEE

Meth is often used with other drugs. Some meth users combine meth with heroin and call it a speedball. Biker's coffee is popular with young city-dwellers and corporate professionals who mix meth with their coffee.[3]

Figure 2.2 Fresno Meth Task Force investigators examine the charred ruins of a meth super lab that exploded in flames near Madeira, California. © Tomas Ovalle/AP Images

THWARTING THE SUPPLY OF
ANHYDROUS AMMONIA

Anhydrous ammonia is another key ingredient in meth manufacturing. In most farm states, authorities say there is a break-in at an anhydrous ammonia tank almost every night. About 82 tons (19,844 gallons) of it was stolen from one Kansas farmer alone. It takes only a few dozen gallons to make a big batch of meth.[23]

States are working to cut off the supply of anhydrous ammonia to meth makers. Iowa has a successful lock program for farmers to secure tanks against theft, and some companies are marketing a solution that dyes the colorless gas a pinkish hue. This dye leaves stains on the clothes and skin, and could help law enforcement track meth manufacturers. Other anhydrous ammonia companies are adding calcium nitrate to it, which in theory competes with lithium during the cooking process so that meth cannot be produced. As of 2006, an Oklahoma law states that *any* possession of anhydrous ammonia in unapproved containers is considered sufficient evidence of intent to manufacture meth.[23]

SMURFING

Over the past 15 years, federal and state meth laws have severely restricted the ingredients and supplies necessary to make meth. These laws have included limiting the amount of ephedrine or pseudoephedrine-containing medication that a person could purchase. Some states only allowed a purchase of three packages at a time. A loophole in the previous meth laws did not include limits on cold and allergy medicines sold in blister packs (plastic bubbles with foil backing). Illegal meth makers seem to always be one step ahead of lawmakers, and "smurfing" is an example of this.[23]

Smurfing is the slang term for driving from one store to the next to buy packages of cold medicines and other meth-making supplies. (The term is named after the little blue

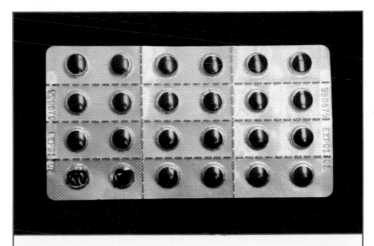

Figure 2.3 Meth producers often "smurf," or hoard, over-the-counter cold medicines sold in blister packs to obtain ephedrine. New laws make this illegal. U.S. Drug Enforcement Administration

cartoon characters who gathered items in similar ways.) The goal is to buy hundreds or thousands of these over-the-counter medicines without arousing the suspicion of store clerks. Stores that sell these products have to keep sales records for these medicines, and they are trained to report any suspicious buying patterns to the police. Three packages at each store and unlimited purchases of blister packs, multiplied by dozens of stores equals a lot of meth precursors.[10, 11]

Sometimes meth abusers hire themselves out as smurfs, and trade the pills for meth. Other times it is the meth cooks themselves who do the smurfing. According to Robert Pennal, head of the Fresno Meth Task Force in California, smurfs punch the pills out of the blister packs and put them in plastic bags while saving the empty packs. Whoever hired them wants to see the actual packs to make sure of the product they are receiving. The smurfs turn over their receipts, and the drug dealer often pays them triple their "investment" in return. In larger scale operations, sophisticated pill-punching machines are used to remove the thousands of pills from their packaging.

A new law passed in 2006 might signal the end of smurfing. Among other things, it eliminates the blister pack loophole and puts all cold medicines behind locked cabinets to deter meth manufacturers.[10, 11]

3

The Properties of Methamphetamine

Methamphetamine can either exist as a "left-handed" molecule named *l*-methamphetamine or a "right-handed" molecule called *d*-methamphetamine. The left and right meth molecules are mirror images of one another. Mirror images represent one same molecule but with different arrangements in space. Such arrangements may not be superimposed. One's right and left hands are an example of mirror images. A helpful way to remember their meanings is as the "*d*rug" or "*l*egal" forms of methamphetamine. The *d*- form of meth has a strong stimulant effect on the brain; its effects on the brain are about three to four times more **potent** than those from the *l*- form.[2, 9]

Due to differences in **potency**, *l*-methamphetamine provides medicinal benefits without any of the addictive potential contained in the illegal *d*-methamphetamine. The *l*- form of methamphetamine is used in some cold medicines, such as Vicks Inhaler, an over-the-counter nasal decongestant. However, to avoid confusion with the illegal version of meth, the manufacturer calls the active ingredient desoxyephedrine.[2]

POWDER, ROCK, PILLS: THE FORMS OF METHAMPHETAMINE

Methamphetamine comes in three forms: a crystalline powder, rock-like chunks, and pills or capsules.

Crystalline Powder

Meth in powder form is typically a white to tan color, but illegally produced meth powder can be yellow, pink, blue, or green depending on the method of manufacture. Red-colored pseudoephedrine tablets can produce a pink meth powder. A bluish tint may come from the use of camper fuel as a solvent. Green meth could be made from green gun scrubber, purchased in sporting goods and hardware stores. Powdered meth can sometimes smell like rotten eggs or urine, and has a bitter taste. A meth lab can be identified by these odors.[2, 7, 14]

Rock

Known as ice, glass, and crystal, these names describe the form of meth that looks like clear, chunky ice or fragments of glass of various sizes. This form tends to be colorless, but can have blue-white coloring. The smoke produced by heating these glassy looking fragments for inhalation is odorless

THE METHAMPHETAMINE MOLECULE

The *l* stands for levo, from the Latin word *laevus* that means "on the left side." The Latin word *dexter* means "on the right side," and is represented by a *d*.[9]

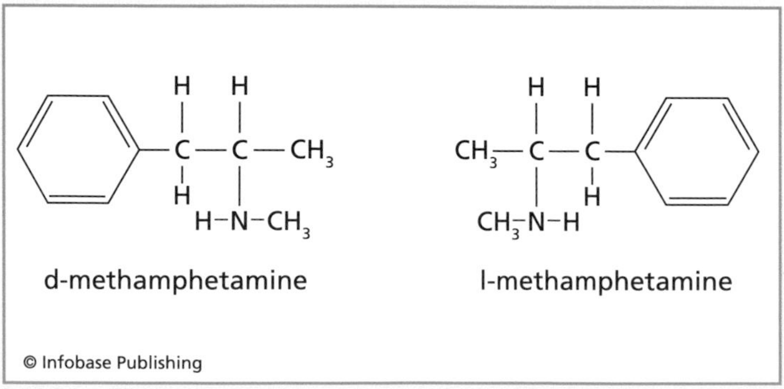

d-methamphetamine   l-methamphetamine

© Infobase Publishing

Figure 3.1 *The chemical structure of d-methamphetamine and l-methamphetamine are mirror images of each other.*

Figure 3.2 One common form of methamphetamine is powder.
U.S. Drug Enforcement Administration

in most cases. From now on, the book will identify this type
of meth as crystal meth or ice.[13]

Pills

The least common form of meth is as a pill or tablet. One
type of meth tablet is reddish-brown and weighs about 90
milligrams (about one-fourth the size of an aspirin). Because
there is no regulation or quality control for illegal drugs,
these pills vary widely in strength. For example, in 2000, an
illegal shipment of these pills was confiscated in California.
Only about 25 percent of each pill was actually meth. The
majority was caffeine.[2]

ROUTES OF EXPOSURE AND
DURATION OF EFFECTS

The way meth enters the body determines its effects. The
crystalline powder can be snorted, eaten, or smoked. It can

Figure 3.3 Methamphetamine in crystalline form is very potent and often called "ice." U.S. Drug Enforcement Administration

be dissolved in a beverage and drunk, or dissolved in water or alcohol and injected. The rock-like form of meth is smoked. Pills are swallowed.[7]

Smoking and Injecting

Smoking and injecting meth delivers a fast and **intoxicating** high. Meth's effects are felt within 10 to 30 *seconds*. Users describe this immediate and intense **rush** or "flash" as extremely pleasurable. This sensation lasts only a few minutes, but the meth user can still feel a sense of euphoric intoxication for 12 to 14 hours or more. After the initial rush, there is typically a state of high agitation known as "tweaking" that in some individuals can lead to rages and violent behavior.[6, 7, 14, 24]

When crystal meth is heated, it gives off vapors (smoke) that can be inhaled through the lungs. Ice is smoked in a glass pipe or an empty light bulb, and it leaves either a milky or black residue inside the glass, depending on the way it was made. The residue left in the glass can be re-smoked.[2, 13]

When meth in crystalline powder form is heated, it easily dissolves in water or alcohol and can then be injected. Meth injection is as risky as using any other intravenous drug. Sharing needles can spread HIV, the virus that causes AIDS (acquired immunodeficiency syndrome), as well as hepatitis B and C.[11, 13, 16]

These routes bypass the digestive process and directly travel to the central nervous system (the brain) via the bloodstream. Because of this fast-acting and direct route to the nervous system, high doses of inhaled and injected drugs can be

A CUPPA JOE

Caffeine is the most widely used legal stimulant in the world. On a daily basis, 80 percent of Americans ingest some form of caffeine. The average adult consumption is about two cups of coffee per day.[9]

Source	Caffeine Content (approximate)
Coffee, brewed (drip)	60–180 mg per 8-oz cup
Coffee, instant	30–120 mg per 8-oz cup
Coffee, decaffeinated	2–5 mg per 8-oz cup
Tea, iced	67–76 mg per 12-oz cup
Chocolate milk	2–7 mg per 8-oz cup
Milk chocolate (Hershey's)	10 mg per 1.5 oz
Jolt	71 mg per 12 oz
Coca-Cola	46 mg per 12 oz
Mountain Dew	54 mg per 12 oz
7-Up, ginger ale, most root beers	0 mg per 12 oz

Figure 3.4 Users often ingest ice by smoking it in a glass pipe.
© Tim Wright/AP Images

more harmful and more addicting over time. In addition, an addictive cycle is generated as the user seeks to re-experience that initial short-lived rush by taking meth with greater doses and frequency.

Eating and Snorting

Oral and intranasal meth use produces a long-lasting **euphoria**—a high—but not an intense rush. This high can last anywhere from 6 to 12 hours. It takes more time for the high to take effect as well, about three to five minutes for snorting and about 15 to 20 minutes for oral ingestion. Snorting crystalline meth powder is also called *railing*, and with long-term use can damage the inside of the nose or cause infection. Users of low doses of meth taken orally obtain effects within 30 to 60 minutes. The euphoric effects are less intense after eating or snorting meth, and require more time to take effect, because the drug first has to go through the digestive process before it hits the bloodstream to be carried to the central nervous system.[2, 7, 9]

EXCRETION

How does methamphetamine get out of the body? The average **half-life** of methamphetamine is about 12 hours. This means it takes about 12 hours for half the amount of meth snorted, swallowed, smoked, or injected to be processed and excreted through the body's natural exits, such as through sweating, urinating, or moving the bowels.[2, 9]

The main way that meth exits the body is through **renal** excretion, also known as urination. The pH of the user's urine will determine how quickly the meth exits the body. The pH is a measure of the acidity or alkalinity of the urine, or any solution, for that matter, where two or more substances are mixed together. The more acidic the urine, the faster meth will exit the body. Acidic urine can speed up the exit process to seven hours instead of 12. Basic (alkaline) urine can slow down meth's excretion by increasing its half-life to 30 hours.[2, 9]

Some illegal meth users drink vinegar or cranberry juice, both of which are very acidic, to try to cleanse themselves of methamphetamines before a drug test. However, even low doses of meth produce a positive urine test for about 24 hours after taking the drug. High-dose users can test positive for meth for two to four days after their last use.[2, 9]

DOSE

It is important to note that any substance—whether an illegal drug or something like everyday water—can benefit or harm a person depending upon its quantity and potency (strength). High doses of a substance can produce very different effects from low doses. Water is necessary for human life, but drinking extreme amounts of it in a short period of time disrupts the **electrolyte** and other critical balances in the body with negative consequences. The methamphetamine drug Desoxyn is beneficial at low doses, but high doses of meth can cause violence and psychosis.[9] Also, size does matter: A person who weighs 100 pounds may experience deleterious or even fatal effects from the same amount of drug taken without adverse effect by someone who weighs 175 pounds.

PURITY AND PRICE

The purer the drug, the more potent it is. The more potent a drug, the more intense are its effects. The more intensely a drug effects someone, the more it potentially addictive it is. Superlabs produce the purest and most potent meth because they have trained chemists making the drug. Depending on the method used, the purity of the meth from superlabs ranges from 80 to 90 percent. Small-scale labs produce meth with much lower purity.[20, 21]

Ice is purer than powdered meth. To make more money, powdered meth is diluted, or "cut," with other ingredients and chemicals. This decreases the purity but increases the total amount of product available to sell. In 2005, the purity of street meth averaged about 54 percent, and contained such substances as baking soda, Epsom salts, quinine (a malaria drug), mannitol (a sugar alternative), ether (a toxic solvent), insecticides (a poison), monosodium glutamate (a preservative), photo developer (a toxic solvent), and strychnine (a poison). Heavy meth users may even prefer these additives because the impurities can give a more intense rush. It is important to remember that it is never possible to know the exact strength or purity of the meth, even if the meth is obtained from a familiar supplier.[2, 13, 20, 21]

The purity of meth has risen and fallen over the years.[25, 26] This reflects a basic supply and demand market. When the key chemicals needed to make meth are not as readily available and therefore are more costly, purity falls because the cooks need to bolster production by adding other substances to the meth. In true market fashion, the price usually goes up during these

METH WEIGHTS AND PRICES IN 2004–2005

An average dose of meth is about a quarter of a gram. Because of ice's intensity, smaller doses provide bigger highs; a gram of ice can provide 10 to 25 hits (doses) of meth. Heavy meth users take three or more grams of meth at a time. Notice how an ounce of gold compares with an ounce of meth.[2, 4, 10, 11, 14, 25, 26]

Dose	Weight	Cost
Quarter	1/4 gram (0.01 ounce)	$20–$80
Half	1/2 gram (0.02 ounce)	$40–$80
Gram	1 gram (0.04 ounce)	$60–$300*
Teenager	1/16 ounce (1.8 grams)	$120–$500
8-Ball	1/8 ounce (3.5 grams)	$100–$250**
Ounce of Meth	1.00 ounce	$1,200–$1,700
Ounce of Gold	1.00 ounce	$500
Pound of Ice	16 ounces	$9,000–$13,000

*Highest retail prices for one gram: Honolulu, Miami, Detroit, and New York City

**Lowest retail prices for one-eighth ounce: Los Angeles, San Diego, and Phoenix

Sources: Community Epidemiology Work Group. NIH Publication No. 06-5878 (2006). NIH Publication No. 05-5280 (2005). Bethesda, MD: National Institute on Drug Abuse.

Gahlinger, Paul M., M.D. *Illegal Drugs*. New York: Penguin Group, 2004.

Johnson, Dirk. *Meth: America's Home-Cooked Menace*. Center City, Minnesota: Hazelden, 2005.

The Stonewall Project. "Weights and Measurements of Meth." Available online. URL: http://www.tweaker.org. Downloaded July 2006.

times. This pattern has occurred each time the government has regulated meth's precursors over the years.

The price of meth also depends upon the amount purchased and where in the country it is sold. Overall, the price of meth has declined since the 1980s, but for illicit meth manufacturers, it is still a profitable business. A superlab making an average amount of meth—100 pounds—can earn the manufacturer about $4 million when sold on the street. For the smaller labs, an investment of about $1,500 in ingredients can be turned into $15,000 in meth sales, a tenfold increase.[2, 11]

4

Methamphetamine and the Brain's Pleasure Center

". . . Young people need to know that maybe for a minute you'll be skinny and full of energy, but . . . here is my story for young people to consider. It takes everything I have to walk a flight of stairs. My lungs are destroyed. I have no control over my bladder—I pee my pants all the time. I can't take a bowel movement without a laxative."

Penny took meth for about four years.[10]

THE METH ROLLER COASTER RIDE

The physical and psychological experiences from meth are often compared to a roller coaster ride. The euphoric intensity accompanied by a rush of exhilaration, energy, alertness, and a sense of invincibility are felt along the highest peaks of the ride. Meth produces an extreme sense of well-being that is usually associated with a sense of accomplishment, love, or some other highly rewarding external source of satisfaction and fulfillment. These effects are temporary and short-lived, yet the lows that follow are of matching intensity and duration, including extreme fatigue, disorientation, depression, and **anhedonia** (an inability to feel pleasure).[9]

METH FOOLS THE BRAIN

The body produces natural stimulants that control the ups and downs of our **biorhythms** (the body's natural cycles) such as sleep

43

needs, mood, or hunger signals. For example, everyone has probably experienced epinephrine rushing through the body. Epinephrine is also known as adrenaline, and is produced by the adrenal glands to create the familiar flight-or-fight response the body experiences when confronted with a dangerous or threatening situation. During this response, the body speeds up all necessary bodily functions to protect us from a perceived harm or to help us to act quickly in an emergency. A thrilling roller coaster ride stimulates the release of epinephrine in the body, creating a rush of sensations.[16]

Methamphetamine provokes the body into creating these types of stimulating body sensations. It does this by fooling the brain into increasing its release and supply of stimulating chemicals. In the case of epinephrine, the meth user is able to artificially stimulate the brain to re-create the energizing rush of feelings, like a racing heart and hyperalertness, that occur normally during a fight-or-flight situation.[16]

Meth affects other of our body's natural stimulants as well. Norepinephrine assists in the biorhythms of sleeping and waking. A common pattern for most people is to feel more energetic and more able to concentrate in the mornings and to feel more tired and mentally unfocused in the late afternoon. Meth allows temporary control over these natural rhythms by decreasing fatigue and increasing wakefulness.[16]

Our body's natural stimulants also decrease appetite and hunger. The reason for this may be related to the fight-or-flight response: As the body mobilizes to defend itself, all digestive and other nonessential processes get turned off while essential parts get turned on, namely the brain, blood, and heart, so that physical and mental awareness are increased.[16]

Everyone is unique, both in personality and their personal biochemistry. Not everyone experiences pleasurable sensations from stimulants. Just like some people do not like roller coaster rides and find their effects unpleasant, some people do not like the effects from stimulants.

THE EFFECTS OF METH ON THE
CENTRAL NERVOUS SYSTEM

Drugs do not contain highs; they trigger highs. The potential for feeling high exists naturally within the human nervous system, and countless options for getting high without taking drugs exist. Indeed, pleasure is a genuine physiological sensation. For example, the "runner's high" is a natural physiological response caused by the release of endogenous chemicals, dopamines. Small children love to get dizzy and disoriented by spinning wildly in circles. Many people go skydiving, fall in love, paint, meditate . . . the list is endless.[16]

Methamphetamine triggers a high via the central nervous system (CNS). The CNS controls the functions of the brain and the spinal cord. There are billions of nerve cells (neurons) within the CNS. A neuron is composed of a cell body; this contains the nucleus that is the director in charge of the neuron. To move a finger to scratch an itch from a bug bite, the neurons responsible for moving your finger need to communicate with each other. Dendrites and axons are fibers on neurons that act like messengers. The axons of one neuron and the dendrites of another neuron are very close but cannot quite touch. These spaces between neurons are called synapses, and because of this distance, the neurons cannot make contact with each other. A neuron releases chemical messengers, called neurotransmitters, from its axon to fill this gap and communicate with another neuron.[7, 27]

Neurotransmitters can be visualized as keys that unlock and open doors on neurons. These doors are called receptors and are located on the dendrites of a neuron. It is through this "key" and "lock" system that messages are conveyed throughout the CNS.

Most receptors are precisely attuned to accept only one type of neurotransmitter key. There are thousands of receptors in the body that will only open for particular neurotransmitters. The primary job of a neurotransmitter is to cross the

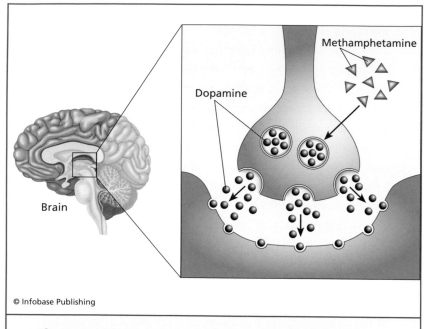

© Infobase Publishing

Figure 4.1 Methamphetamine creates a sensation of pleasure by causing neurons in the brain to release excess dopamine.

synapse, find its receptor on the dendrites of the neighboring neuron, and unlock it. The dendrite then delivers the chemical message to the nucleus of its neuron. Message delivered!

Each neurotransmitter is responsible for a particular action. Some stimulate and some inhibit. Some neurotransmitters are responsible for movement. Others are needed for memory or for feeling emotions. Once the message has been delivered, the neurotransmitter is either destroyed or reabsorbed into the neuron that released it. This whole process is called neurotransmission.

THE NEUROTRANSMITTER DOPAMINE

"At a purely chemical level, every experience humans find enjoyable—whether listening to music, embracing a lover, or savoring chocolate—amounts to little more than an explosion of dopamine in the brain, as exhilarating and short-lived as a firecracker."[9]

Dopamine is the chemical in our body most fundamental to promoting the experience of pleasure. This neurotransmitter comes from the reward center of the brain (rewarding the person with high levels of positive, loving, pleasurable feelings). It is responsible for creating euphoria and uplifting emotions and mood. Dopamine helps control the limbic system, a part of the brain associated with basic needs and emotions, for example hunger, pain, pleasure, satisfaction, sex, and instinctive motivation. Dopamine is also responsible for many of the body's activities, including motor coordination.[9]

Eventually, this sense of well-being from dopamine wears off. The "key"—dopamine—that was "locked" in the receptors is released and sent back to the neuron that sent it in the first place. This neuron stores the dopamine for future use, a kind of recycling. Basically, this is how all receptors and neurotransmitters work in the body.[7]

THE METH HIGH: DOPAMINE

Methamphetamine's powerful effects come from its impact on the brain's reward, or pleasure, center. Meth does not directly release dopamine. It attaches itself to dopamine receptor sites and fools neurons into releasing large quantities of dopamine. This accounts for the intense rush a user experiences from meth.[7, 11]

In addition, meth prevents dopamine from being recycled. Instead, dopamine is active in the body for much longer, explaining the extra long duration of the meth high. The drug does this by blocking (inhibiting) the dopamine transporter involved in its reabsorption (reuptake) into the original neuron that sent it. Transporters are places on neurons that reabsorb the dopamine after it has completed its job. As a result, more dopamine becomes available to the brain. This extra dopamine, in turn, activates an even greater number of dopamine receptors. This increased release of dopamine is primarily responsible for the intensity and duration of meth-amphetamine's effects.[9]

In lab animal experiments conducted by Dr. Richard Rawson, director of UCLA's Integrated Substance Abuse Program, sex caused dopamine levels to increase to 200 units and cocaine caused levels to rise to 350 units. With methamphetamine, dopamine levels jumped to about 1,250 units. Overall, this study showed that meth causes about 12 times as much feelings of pleasure as sex, food, and other activities, including the use of other illegal stimulant drugs. Rawson noted that all illegal drugs of abuse release dopamine, but that methamphetamine "produces the mother of all dopamine releases."[11]

NOREPINEPHRINE AND ANOREXIA

In a similar, though somewhat less substantial way, methamphetamine affects norepinephrine levels in the brain.

METHAMPHETAMINE VERSUS COCAINE

Meth and cocaine share similar stimulating effects because they provoke excessive dopamine to collect in the brain. However, meth stays in the body longer than cocaine. This results in a longer lasting high for meth, but means that meth has more time to damage neurons in the brain as well.[7, 11]

Methamphetamine	Cocaine
• man-made	• plant-derived
• smoking produces a high that lasts 8 to 24 hours	• smoking produces a high that lasts 20 to 30 minutes
• 50% of the drug is removed from the body in 12 hours	• 50% of the drug is removed from the body in 1 hour
• limited medical use	• used as a local anesthetic in some surgical procedures

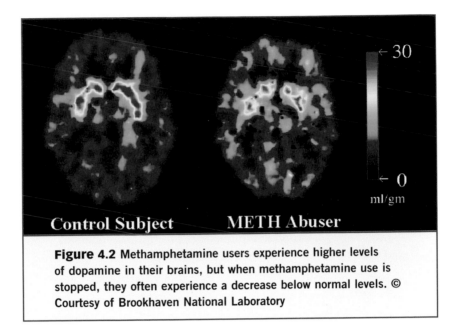

← 30

← 0

ml/gm

Control Subject   METH Abuser

Figure 4.2 Methamphetamine users experience higher levels of dopamine in their brains, but when methamphetamine use is stopped, they often experience a decrease below normal levels. © Courtesy of Brookhaven National Laboratory

Many receptors for the neurotransmitter norepinephrine are found in a small section of the brain stem called the locus coeruleus, a part of the brain that integrates sensory messages from the eyes, ears, and other sense organs. Common reactions to norepinephrine release in the body are increased heart rate and body temperature. Amazingly, this part of the brain has only a few thousand nerve cells, but is connected to about a third of the entire brain. The persistent lack of appetite resulting from a meth high is probably due to the release of this neurotransmitter in the hypothalamus "satiety" section of the brain. This would communicate to the brain that it is satisfied and does not need any food to sustain it. Meth users are often described as looking emaciated and skeletal; this constant release of norepinephrine can lead to **anorexia**.[9] As a result, some teens use meth to lose weight. This is more common with teenage girls.

SHORT-TERM EFFECTS

Even small amounts of methamphetamine can cause such physical effects as insomnia, loss of appetite, increased physical activity, racing heart, increased sexual libido, increased rate of breathing, tremors, elevated blood pressure and body temperature, dilation of pupils (meth users might wear sunglasses due to a sensitivity to light, whether indoors or outside), convulsions, nausea, vomiting, stomach cramps, and diarrhea.[7, 16]

Psychological effects include euphoria, alertness, obsession with details, anxiety, irritability, rage, aggressiveness, depression, paranoia, hallucinations, psychosis, and anhedonia. Remember, these psychological and physical effects can last anywhere from six to 14 hours or more, depending on the route of exposure, dose, and purity of the meth used.[7, 16]

Teens report feeling uninhibited, in control, confident, and energetic after taking meth.[1] Yet the high that meth brings is temporary. When meth users come down from their high, the negative effects are so intense that this experience is called *crashing*. The paradox of meth is that the sought-after euphoric effects of the meth high quickly turn into their opposite. Users need more and more meth to achieve and maintain the same high they felt when they first used meth. Research indicates that this can happen after using meth only one or two times.[7, 9] Eventually, users need meth just to feel any type of pleasure whatsoever. Some meth users try to alleviate the negative effects of crashing by taking other drugs such as cocaine or heroin. This vicious cycle of chasing after a meth high to feel normal and to escape meth's crushing aftereffects is what makes meth an extremely addictive drug compared to any other stimulants.[9, 16]

TOLERANCE

Tolerance can be defined as the need for increasing doses of a drug over time to maintain the same effect achieved at previous lower doses. The body becomes tolerant to the effects of meth *within minutes*.[7, 9] Remember, after smoking or injecting meth, the user experiences an intense explosion of dopamine, experienced as a euphoric high. Meth users try to maintain that high by using ever-increasing quantities of meth, or by switching to a faster-acting way of using, such as moving from snorting to injecting. Some abusers go on a binge known as a "meth run," injecting a gram (1,000 mg) of meth every two to three hours until the user runs out of the drug or is too intoxicated to continue.[2] This can last for several days or even weeks. To compare, a medicinal dose of legal methamphetamine, Desoxyn, is about five to 15 milligrams (mg) per day. This means a user on a meth run is taking approximately 800 times the therapeutic dose of meth each day.[2, 9] (Approximate illegal dose of 1,000 mg times every three hours [eight times a day] divided by an average of 10 mg, the therapeutic dose of meth.)

There are two ways to understand how a person can develop tolerance to meth.[9] First, methamphetamine depletes the neurotransmitter norepinephrine from the body. As the brain's supply of norepinephrine dwindles, the user needs more and more meth to maintain a consistent high. This tolerance can happen *after only one or two doses of meth*. Secondly, **ketosis** causes tolerance. Ketosis is a by-product of not eating for long periods of time. Not only does this produce very bad breath, but when a person stops eating, it changes the body's metabolism, causing the urine to become more acidic. As we learned in Chapter Three, the more acidic the urine, the more methamphetamine is excreted in the urine. This causes the user to need more and more meth to achieve the same high.

BINGING, TWEAKING, AND CRANK BUGS

Many meth users go on "binge and crash" runs for three to five days and then crash, sleeping for one or two days. During these binges, users often become agitated and feel "wired." Their behavior becomes unpredictable. They may be friendly and calm one moment, then angry and terrified the next, prone to out-of-control rages, delusions, paranoia, and violence. This phase of the meth high is called *tweaking*. Tweakers become hyperactive, obsessed with details, and intensely focused, and feel compelled to repeat meaningless tasks, such as taking apart and reassembling clocks, stereos, and other types of machinery. The release of high amounts of the body's fight-or-flight chemicals, epinephrine (adrenaline) and norepinephrine, is thought to cause this tweaking effect in a meth user.

Tweakers may also have a strong sensation of bugs crawling beneath their skin, a disorder known medically as **formication** but more often referred to as "crank bugs." Meth users can pick obsessively at these invisible "bugs," creating unsightly oozing sores and scabs on their faces and bodies.[5, 7, 11, 24]

5

The Long-Term Health Effects of Methamphetamine

The temporary physical and psychological effects from meth can turn into long-term, permanent effects that last a lifetime. For instance, meth dramatically affects a person's decision-making abilities. The temporary effect of increased libido leads meth users to engage in risky, unprotected sex. A recent study of 19,000 men in Los Angles showed that new **HIV** infections were three times higher among methamphetamine users than among nonusers.[28] Also, HIV and other infectious diseases like hepatitis B and C are spread among injection drug users mainly by sharing syringes and needles. Multiple injections also scar the skin and the veins. Because of the eventual reversal of meth's effects, long-term methamphetamine use is associated with *decreased* sexual functioning and libido, at least in men.[9, 11]

Heavy use of meth lowers immune function (the body's ability to heal). Meth raises blood pressure, and over time weakens and destroys blood vessels. This cuts off blood flow to parts of the body. Crank bug sores often take a long time to heal, and meth users' skin in general loses it elasticity and shine. Chronic meth users tend to forget about basic self-care, such as brushing teeth, taking a shower, eating, sleeping, or wearing clean clothes. All of these combine to dramatically age the body, making a meth user look much older than he or she really is.[7]

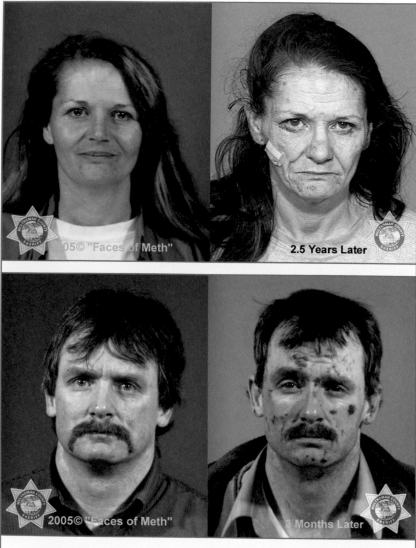

Figure 5.1 Methamphetamine dramatically ages those who abuse it and ravages their bodies. © Multnomah County Sheriff's Office

The illegal manufacture of meth can also have health hazards. The chemicals involved can also damage internal organs and are known carcinogens. It is easy for a meth cooker to breathe the solvent fumes and gas by-products used in making meth. The damage to the lungs, skin, and eyes from chronic exposure to meth lab chemicals also can be instantaneous, causing blindness and respiratory illnesses.[20]

Meth's effects on the brain can also affect social functioning. Many chronic meth users drop out of school or employment altogether. It is impossible to keep up with classes or hold down a job when one is awake and high for days at a time and then, exhausted, needing to sleep for several days. Reports of teen meth users stealing from their families and friends are commonplace, injuring relationships and trust. And, of course, methamphetamine is illegal unless prescribed by a physician, and is punishable with heavy fines and prison.

METH DAMAGES THE BRAIN . . . PERMANENTLY?

For 20 years, scientific evidence has shown that long-term use of meth depletes supplies of dopamine by damaging dopamine receptors in the brain.[24] Studies indicate that this brain damage can be permanent. Long-term meth users may develop life-long problems with verbal skills, memory, and may even develop Parkinson's disease, an incurable nervous disorder with symptoms of trembling hands and extreme muscle stiffness.[6, 11]

According to the National Institute on Drug Abuse (NIDA), animal studies show as much as 50 percent of the dopamine-producing cells in the brain can be damaged after long-term exposure to relatively low levels of methamphetamine. In other animal studies, a single high dose of the drug has been shown to damage nerve endings in the dopamine-containing regions of the brain. The nerve endings do not die, but do not grow back to their original sizes. Researchers also have found that serotonin (another neurotransmitter) and norepinephrine-containing nerve cells may be damaged as extensively.[7, 8, 9, 17, 24, 29]

It is often difficult to compare animal studies to humans because very high doses of drugs are used in animal studies. However, scientists using brain-imaging techniques have studied the brains of human meth users. They have discovered that

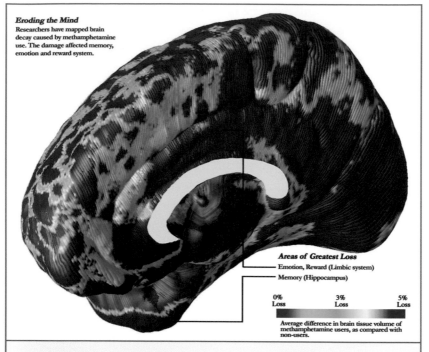

Eroding the Mind
Researchers have mapped brain decay caused by methamphetamine use. The damage affected memory, emotion and reward system.

Areas of Greatest Loss
— Emotion, Reward (Limbic system)
— Memory (Hippocampus)

| 0% Loss | 3% Loss | 5% Loss |

Average difference in brain tissue volume of methamphetamine users, as compared with non-users.

Figure 5.2 Brain damage due to methamphetamine can be long-lasting or even permanent. © Paul Thompson, Kiralee Hayashi, Arthur Toga, Edythe London/UCLA

even three years after long-term meth users had quit using the drug, their dopamine neurons remained damaged.[7]

Dr. Nora Volkow, director of NIDA, studied brain scans taken of meth users who had been drug free for more than 14 months. The meth users had memory loss and other psychological and physical side effects. The results showed that although most of the damaged dopamine receptors had grown back, the **sober** meth users still did not show much improvement in their cognitive abilities—their memory, judgment, ability to think clearly, or motor coordination skills—*even after a year of being off the drug*. Additional brain studies show that the damaged brain cells may never completely grow back to their original size. [17, 29]

A 2004 study led by Dr. Paul Thompson, an expert on brain mapping at the University of California, Los Angeles, showed how the brain's center for making new memories, the hippocampus, lost 8 percent of its tissue in meth users. This is comparable to the brain losses seen in early Alzheimer's patients. The study compared 22 people in their 30s who had been using methamphetamine for 10 years, mostly by smoking it with 21 non-drug taking people of the same age. On average, the meth users smoked an average of four grams a week and said they had been high on 19 of the 30 days before the study began. The meth abusers fared significantly worse on memory tests than did healthy people the same age.[30] In 2005, the average street price of four grams of meth was about $200 to $250, which means these meth users were smoking about $800 to $1,000 of meth each month.[10, 25, 26]

Although more studies are needed to clarify what long-term effects are seen at specific dosage levels and with different routes of exposure, these results offer a strong connection between damage to dopamine nerve endings and negative long-term physical and psychological effects experienced by meth users.

BRAIN CRAVINGS FOR METH

Meth's damage to dopamine in the brain means less dopamine is naturally available to the body. The brain becomes dependent upon constant meth intake to stimulate the supply of dopamine. Because the brain loses its ability to manufacture its own, it begins to crave dopamine when a meth user does not supply the drug. This is a major reason why users become so quickly tolerant and then addicted to meth. Without the drug to supply dopamine to the brain, meth users are unable to experience pleasure (anhedonia). At this stage, meth users can become deeply depressed and even suicidal. Even those who want to quit meth have great difficulties in overcoming these feelings, and resort to meth to escape them.[2, 10, 16]

METH MOUTH

A very common and visible sign of long-term meth use is extreme tooth decay, also known as "meth mouth." Users with meth mouth have blackened, stained, or rotting teeth, which often can't be saved. False teeth, dentures, and other dental products are normally reserved for older people who have lost their teeth. Many short-term meth users, including teens, are receiving this type of dental work to replace lost teeth. Some dentists have seen as significant a tooth loss in four-month meth users as those who have used meth for four years.

As discussed, meth damages blood vessels and decreases blood flow to all parts of the body. This includes the blood supply needed by the gums and mouth to stay healthy. Meth use causes these oral tissues to decay. In addition, meth use dries out the mouth, a condition called **xerostomia**. Saliva protects the teeth from harsh acids in the mouth. Without enough saliva to neutralize these acids, the teeth and gums are eaten away, causing weak spots that are susceptible to cavities. The cavities are worsened by the lifestyle of meth users: eating a lot of sugary foods and drinks, compulsively grinding their teeth, and neglecting to regularly brush and floss their teeth.[7, 11]

THE HEART, LUNGS, AND BODY TEMPERATURE

Intravenous meth users experience a high within 30 seconds of injecting the drug. The reason for this speedy reaction is because once injected into the bloodstream, meth travels straight to the heart. It causes veins and arteries to constrict, which then reduces blood flow and elevates blood pressure, leading to increased body temperature, faster heartbeat, and possible blood clotting. High doses and frequency of meth use can increase body temperature (called **hyperthermia**) to dangerous levels, causing convulsions or even death. The National Institute on Drug Abuse reports body temperatures as high as 108 degrees Fahrenheit following meth use.[7, 13]

Long-term users also raise their risk of arrhythmia (meaning irregular heartbeat), heart attacks, and cardiovascular collapse.

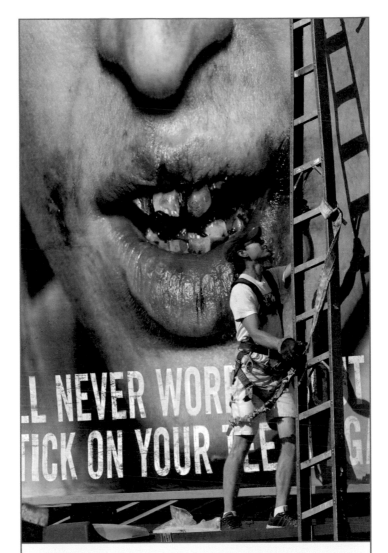

Figure 5.3 Campaigns against methamphetamine abuse have highlighted the drug's destructive effects with graphic depictions of "meth mouth," like the one displayed on this Montana billboard. © Robin Loznak/AP Images

Methamphetamine can cause inflammation of the heart lining, and also permanently damage the small blood vessels in the brain, which can lead to stroke (bleeding inside the brain).[7, 13]

There is overwhelming and ample evidence that smoke from cigarettes and marijuana contains cancer-causing chemicals and damages the lungs in multiple ways. In similar ways, smoking meth harms the lungs; it is probably the most impure form of intake because the burning of the drug actually causes other toxic by-products that have serious negative affects on the lungs. The ingredients used to make meth (i.e., engine starter fluid, drain cleaner) can actually block blood vessels in the lungs, and, as a result, long-term use can permanently reduce the amount of air the lungs are able to take in. [2, 31]

LONG-TERM PSYCHOLOGICAL EFFECTS

As compared to physical tolerance, there is no tolerance established for the psychological effects of methamphetamine.[9] This leaves meth users very vulnerable to its psychotic effects. Long-time users have been known to develop symptoms of psychosis that mimic **schizophrenia**, including paranoia, aggression, hallucinations, and delusions. Even after stopping the drug, psychotic symptoms can sometimes persist for months or years afterward.[7, 11, 14]

Of a population of 111 patients with chronic methamphetamine psychosis (MAP), 21 patients were selected for a study. Sixteen of these patients had used meth one or more times after a long-term abstinence; when they reused the drug, they experienced an acute, paranoid psychotic state that was almost identical to the psychotic episode they had experienced when first using the drug years before. Four of these patients relapsed following a one-time reuse of meth (of an amount less than what they had initially used). One patient relapsed without even showing signs of having reused meth. The study concluded that chronic meth use can cause long-term "susceptibility to sensitization" to meth. Antipsychotic medications, such as haloperidol, are being used to help meth abusers with these aftereffects.[32]

6

Teenage Trends and Attitudes

Headlines over the last several years have declared a meth epidemic in the United States among adults and teens. An epidemic is an outbreak that spreads more quickly and more extensively among a particular group of people than would be normally expected. Many indicators tell us how meth use and abuse has increased over the past 15 years, both in actual numbers of users and across the country. Admissions to substance abuse treatment centers, drug seizures, meth lab busts, emergency room visits, and national surveys on meth use are among the many ways of verifying just how many people are using and abusing methamphetamines. Yet how many teens are actually using meth?[11, 15, 18. 23]

It may be that describing the meth problem as an epidemic is overstated because the actual number of adults and teens using meth is still far lower than the number using marijuana, cocaine, or heroin. In fact, although there has been an increase in meth use among certain age groups, overall teen meth use has *decreased* over the last several years. Perhaps this is related to recently enacted laws and increased prevention programs aimed at decreasing the supply and demand of the drug. Perhaps other factors contributed to this decline.

IDENTIFYING TEENAGE TRENDS AND ATTITUDES

Adolescent trends in drug use have been tracked for more than 30 years. Researchers use this wealth of data to predict future trends and their possible implications on adolescent health and the general society. Patterns of drug use tend to be inversely related to perceived

METH IS CITED AS BIGGEST DRUG PROBLEM

In a 2005 survey conducted by the National Association of Counties, 58 percent of law enforcement officials cited methamphetamine as their biggest drug problem. Some counties in the Midwest report that more than 75 percent of those *incarcerated* (imprisoned) in their jails are there because of meth. The United Nations identifies meth as the most abused hard drug in the world, with 26 million people addicted to it. That is more than all the cocaine and heroin abusers combined.[11, 33]

health risks. For example, in recent years, as knowledge of the health risks from cigarette smoking has increased, the number of teens who smoke has declined.

The U.S. Department of Health and Human Services (HHS) tracks the nation's substance abuse patterns through three major surveys: the National Survey on Drug Use and Health (NSDUH), the Monitoring the Future Survey (MTF), and the Drug Abuse Warning Network (DAWN). These three surveys address the broad category of "illicit drugs," which includes amphetamines (including methamphetamine and crystal meth), hallucinogens, marijuana, cocaine, heroin, inhalants, and several other substances. The surveys show results about drug use, trends, and attitudes for specific drugs and particular age categories. Marijuana has dominated for almost the entire 30 years, accounting for 50 to 75 percent of all illicit drug use.[19, 34, 35]

Statistical information from these surveys helps the government identify potential drug abuse problem areas in order to set national drug policy and allocate financial resources that target areas of greatest need. Data from these large-scale surveys are also used to develop prevention and treatment campaigns, with particular emphasis on programs aimed at youth aged 12 to 17.

INTERPRETING THE DATA

An important role of the researcher is to interpret statistical information. All statistics need to be assessed with a critical eye, because, on the surface, percentages and rates can sound so "official" that many accept their truth without analyzing the underlying assumptions that generated the statistics in the first place. For instance, it is important to note that the surveys cited here rely on self-reporting, a method that can contribute to underreporting since teens may be reluctant to fully report their illegal drug use.

Also, statistics can sometimes be misleading. In a hypothetical example, a 90 percent increase in teen drug use over a three-year period sounds enormous. However, if the actual number of teens who used the drug went from 10 to 19, and these 19 teens were a part of a population of 250,000 people, this 90 percent increase would hardly seem as impressive. It would still be important to know that teen drug use had increased; this information could be applied in useful ways. It is important to have as much background as possible for the data being presented.

TRENDS IN TEENAGE METH USE

The National Surveys on Drug Use and Health gathered the following information for the the years 2003–2004:[35]

- Each year, more Americans are trying meth. The number of people over the age of 12 who have tried meth in their lifetime in 1994 was 1.8 million; in 1997, it was 5.3 million; in 1999, 9.4 million had tried it, and in 2004, the number was nearly 12 million.

- In 2004, an estimated 1.4 million people aged 12 or older had used methamphetamine in the past year, and 600,000 people had used methamphetamine in the past month.

- In those aged 12 to 17, about 300,000 had tried meth at least once in their lifetime, 163,000 had used meth at least

DEFINITIONS

LIFETIME USE

Both the NSDUH and the MTF define a "lifetime user" as a teen who has used an illicit drug/meth at least once in his or her lifetime.

PAST-YEAR (ANNUAL) USE

This is used to describe a teen who has used meth at least once during the past 365 days.

PAST-MONTH OR CURRENT USER

Both the NSDUH and the MTF define a "current user" as a teen who has used an illicit drug/meth at least once within the month prior to responding to the survey. This is also referred to as "past-month" drug use.

NATIONAL AVERAGE

The results from the sample groups are applied to the entire population of the United States and then presented as a national average.

once in the past year, and 57,000 had used meth in the previous month.

- In the general population of 12 and older, more men than women use meth. However, in those aged 12 to 17, *more women have either tried meth in their lifetime or used it in the past year.* Male and female 12- to 17-year-olds used meth about the same rates over a 30-day period.

- The number of 14- to 15-year-old meth users increased from 2003 to 2004, but decreased for 16 to 17 year olds.

- Less than 1 percent of all 12- to 17-year-olds used meth in 2004. However, that still means 163,000 teens used meth that year.

- As a group, 12- to 17-year-olds used less methamphet-amines in 2004 than in 2003. This is part of a trend of decreased meth use *among teens* seen over the past few years. However, those between the ages of 18 to 25 show a slight increase in meth use.

- The average age of people using meth for the first time is 20.

Monitoring the Future Survey Results[19, 34]

Findings from the 2005 MTF survey tell us more specifically about meth trends among 10th and 12th graders.

Lifetime use

- When analyzing data over the past 15 years, lifetime use (use at least once) of any illicit drug has increased for both 10th and 12th graders.

- According to the survey, half (50 percent) of all American students have tried some type of illicit drug by the time they near high school graduation.

- Since 1999, meth has shown a 45 percent decrease in both 10th and 12th grade lifetime use. *Despite the publicity about the growing meth problem in the country, as a whole, this age group has shown a fairly steady decline in use, according to both the NSDUH and MTF results.*

- Ice was included in the MTF survey beginning in 1990, as it was a new drug introduced at that time. After peaking in 1998, lifetime use of ice (crystal meth) slightly decreased for the next five years among high school seniors, the only age group included in this survey. However, since 2003, ice use has remained level. About the same number of high school seniors report using meth as report using crystal meth at least once in their life-time, according to the 2005 data.

Methamphetamine Use in Past Year Among Persons Aged 12 or Older, by State: 2002, 2003, and 2004

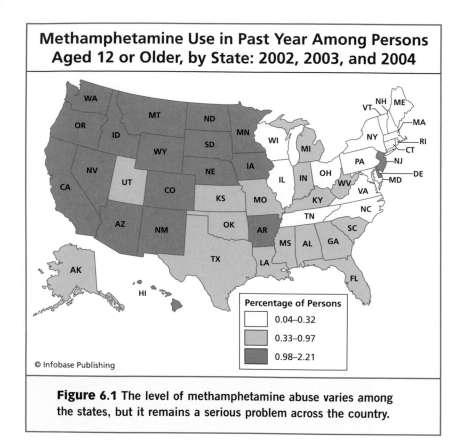

Percentage of Persons

☐	0.04–0.32
☐	0.33–0.97
■	0.98–2.21

© Infobase Publishing

Figure 6.1 The level of methamphetamine abuse varies among the states, but it remains a serious problem across the country.

Past-year and past-month use

- Use of meth and ice in the past year and in the past month follow the lifetime trends of decreasing meth use and increasing crystal meth use.

- Since 1999, the number of 10th and 12th graders who have used meth in the past year and the past month has dropped by 40 to 45 percent.

- The number of high school seniors using ice in the past year has increased nearly 65 percent over the last 15 years (since 1991). Since 2003, crystal meth use has remained steady for both annual and monthly use. (In 2005, annual

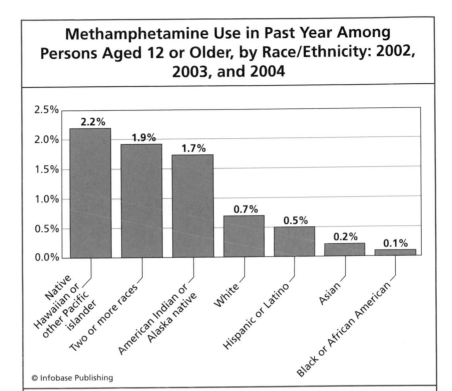

Methamphetamine Use in Past Year Among Persons Aged 12 or Older, by Race/Ethnicity: 2002, 2003, and 2004

© Infobase Publishing

Figure 6.2 People of many different ethnic backgrounds abuse methamphetamine.

use was 2.3 percent.) Past-month use of crystal meth has seen smaller increases, but an increase nonetheless.

- It is important to note that even though ice use is increasing, the same number of high school seniors used meth as used ice in 2005. Interestingly, there were more 10th grade users of meth in 2005 than there were high school senior users of ice. In general, the actual numbers of students using meth is higher than those using crystal meth on an annual basis.

- Annually, women in 10th grade use meth more often than men in 10th grade and women in 12th grade. This means that even though teen use of meth is declining, 10th grade girls are more likely to use meth than their male or older female counterparts. This trend has been evident for the past seven years, since 1999. Male 10th and 12th graders used about the same amount of meth in 2005. This corresponds with the NSDUH data on gender and meth use.

Drug Abuse Warning Network Results[18]

The latest results from DAWN provide estimates on meth-related Emergency Department (ED) visits in 2004. These estimates are based on the general population (i.e. teens *and* adults) unless specified:

- Of the 106 million ED visits during 2004, 2 million are estimated to be drug related. Of those 2 million, about 1.3 million involved the misuse or abuse of illicit drugs or alcohol.

- Methamphetamine was mentioned in 6 percent (73,400) of all illicit drug-related ED visits. As a comparison, cocaine was involved in 30 percent (383,350) and marijuana in 17 percent (215,665) of all illicit drug-related ED visits.

FEMALE TEEN ATHLETES USE LESS DIET DRUGS

The results of a 2004 study called ATHENA (Athletes Targeting Healthy Exercise and Nutrition Alternatives) suggest that female teens who participate in team sports at school tend to have very healthy eating habits and seem deterred from using diet pills and performance-enhancing drugs. The study included 928 female students from 40 participating sports teams at 18 high schools, with an average age of 15.4 years.[36]

- Both amphetamines and methamphetamine are included in the stimulant category, but methamphetamine makes up the majority of ED involvement (over 70 percent).

- Of these meth-related ED visits, 25 percent were checked into the hospital for medical treatment, including intensive care. Half of all meth visits ended in the person being discharged that same day. A very small number were released to the police (less than 5 percent).

- In 2004, patients aged 12 to 17 accounted for about 9 percent of all meth-related ED visits. Patients aged 25–29 had the highest number of meth-related ED visits.

- ED visits vary across the major illicit drugs:
  - 131 visits per 100,000 population for cocaine
  - 73 visits per 100,000 population for marijuana
  - 55 visits per 100,000 population for heroin
  - 25 visits per 100,000 population for methamphetamine

SUBGROUP DIFFERENCES

There are important distinctions in teen meth use based on subgroup variations. Subgroups are defined as gender, rural versus urban (city) areas, a teen's college plans, the different regions of the country, and race/ethnicity. Gender differences have already been noted in the statistics above.

- The 2004 NSDUH reports that teens who live in large, urban areas tended to smoke meth while those living in smaller, rural areas are more likely to inject the drug. This correlates to a higher use of crystal meth (which is most often smoked) in more urban areas than rural areas.[35]

- The 2005 MTF reports:[19, 34]
  - Students who are not college-bound are considerably more likely to be at risk for using illicit drugs. In 2005, 7.3 percent of 10th graders *not* planning on going to

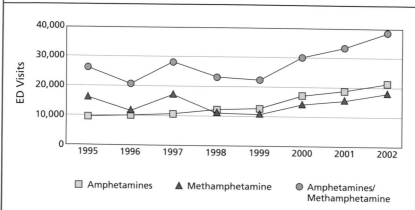

Amphetamines, Methamphetamine, and Amphetamines/Methamphetamine (Combined) ED Visits for the Coterminous U.S., 1995–2002

☐ Amphetamines ▲ Methamphetamine ● Amphetamines/Methamphetamine

Source: Office of Applied Studies, SAMHSA, Drug Abuse Warning Network, 2002 (03/2003 update). Individual estimates for amphetamines and methamphetamine are available on the DAWN Web site, at http://DAWNinfo.samhsa.gov/.

© Infobase Publishing

Figure 6.3 Recent years have marked a steady rise in the number of emergency room visits due to abuse of amphetamines, methamphetamine, or a combination of both drugs.

college used meth in the last year, as compared to 2.2 percent of college-bound students.

- Methamphetamine use began in the Western states in the 1960s, and, as late as 1999, annual use by 12th graders still heavily favored the West. However, by 2005, the 10th and 12th graders in the North Central states had reported the greatest annual use. This correlates to data that shows the largest number of meth lab seizures in the country were in Missouri, Iowa, and Illinois, for example. This regional spread of meth is viewed as another indicator that we are experiencing a "meth epidemic."

- One of the most dramatic changes in meth use is its rise in use by Hispanic teens. Until recently, meth use largely has been defined by white, male users. However, between 1999 and 2005, white male meth users *declined* among both 10th and 12th graders. In contrast, by 2005, the percentage of meth usage among *Hispanic* 10th graders was 72 percent greater than the percentage of meth use among white 10th graders.

- African Americans have consistently shown exceptionally low rates for both meth and crystal meth use.

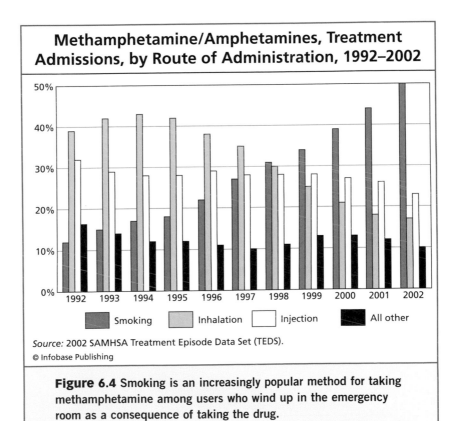

Methamphetamine/Amphetamines, Treatment Admissions, by Route of Administration, 1992–2002

Legend: Smoking, Inhalation, Injection, All other

Source: 2002 SAMHSA Treatment Episode Data Set (TEDS).
© Infobase Publishing

Figure 6.4 Smoking is an increasingly popular method for taking methamphetamine among users who wind up in the emergency room as a consequence of taking the drug.

PREDICTIVE FACTORS: WHY DO SOME TEENS CHOOSE TO USE METHAMPHETAMINE?

Based upon over 25 years of surveys, the Overview of Key Findings portion of the Monitoring the Future Survey has determined that there are seven factors that tend to predict the likelihood of drug use by teenagers: awareness, motivations for use, reassurance about safety, a willingness to break social norms by violating the law, personality type, peer approval/disapproval and parental approval/disapproval. These factors are useful for predicting meth use in teens.[19, 34]

AWARENESS

The media play an important role in creating awareness of illegal drugs, although not always intentionally. From news reports headlining "The Meth Epidemic" to antidrug advertisements to dramatic story lines showing favorite actors using drugs (whether advocating their use or taking an antidrug stance), the media introduces drugs to a mass audience.

EIGHT WARNING SIGNS THAT A FRIEND MAY BE USING METH[1]

- extremely dilated pupils
- dry or bleeding nose and lips
- chronic nasal or sinus problems
- bad breath
- sores on arms and face
- drastic weight loss or anorexia
- an extreme change in school grades
- an extreme change in friends (leaving his or her usual crowd for friends who only get high or are in trouble with the law)

However, a process called *generational forgetting* can fuel drug awareness.[19, 34] Researchers at Monitoring the Future assert that the "speed (meth) kills" slogans of the past are forgotten because the generations who took meth back in the 1960s have been replaced with a younger generation. This younger generation does not know about or remember the adverse effects of meth experienced in the 1960s. According to the MTF, this makes it important to continually pass along information about the potential dangers of methamphetamine from generation to generation. Their statistics suggest that each generation must learn anew to increase their awareness about the hazards of using these drugs. Communities, parents, schools, and lawmakers take this finding seriously, and today continue to build awareness of the consequences of drug use and abuse.

MOTIVATIONS TO USE METH

"Meth made me get out of my shell. I didn't want the feeling to go away." "I felt weightless and had a smile ear to ear." "My life was suddenly perfect, and I was perfect. I didn't want it to end. I stayed up for seven days." "I wanted to lose weight. Meth was a fast way to do it." "Meth makes you feel more powerful, like you can do anything."[1]

There are multiple reasons why teenagers enjoy "getting high," as can be seen from these reactions from teens about their experiences with meth. Others start using meth because they need to study all night or keep up with demanding school and work schedules. Meth is popularly used at all-night parties called *raves*. Some may use meth out of a sense of curiosity or adventure, the desire to "fit in" with a group of friends, or out of boredom. And, for every generation, defiance of parents can be a motivation to use drugs such as meth.

Some teens use meth to deal with depression, anger, anxiety, and family/school problems in attempts to escape from such problems. These "negative" reasons for getting high are the most common in a teen that has underlying psychological issues. This is especially true for adolescents who may substitute drugs as a coping mechanism rather than developing the skills critical to living a full and functional adult life.[16]

REASSURANCE ABOUT THE SAFETY OF METH

When deciding to do something, people weigh the pros and cons—the benefits and the risks—and then make a decision. Experts describe this as weighing the "perceived risks" against the "perceived benefits," and use this framework to gain further insights into teenage trends in drug use.

Studies show that information about the perceived benefits of a drug usually spread much faster along teen grapevines, especially on the Internet, than information about the adverse risks of that drug. It usually takes longer for evidence of a drug's risks (i.e., addictive potential, overdose reactions, etc.) to accumulate and then be disseminated. Thus, when a new drug is introduced to teens, like crystal meth in the 1980s, the drug enjoys a considerable "grace period." During this time, a new drug's benefits are popularized while its consequences are not yet known.[19, 34]

When the perceived risks of using a drug catch up with its perceived benefits, the use of that drug likely will decline. This inverse cause and effect link has been supported by survey results, suggesting that teens who believe a particular drug can harm them are less likely to use that drug. This works in the opposite way as well. Teens who do not perceive any risks about a drug tend to use that drug. Looked at in terms of meth, students who use meth are less likely to disapprove of its use and to see its use as dangerous. [16, 19, 34]

The 2005 MTF survey asked high school seniors about the perceived risks of using crystal meth once or twice.[19, 34]

- Over the 15 year period from 1991 to 2005, there has been a slight decrease in the perceived risk of crystal meth (from 62 percent in 1991 to 55 percent in 2005). This finding is an expected outcome since it corresponds with the slight increase in annual use of crystal meth.

- However, looking only at 2004 and 2005, it is important to note that the perceived risks of using ice actually have increased slightly. It will be interesting to see whether this increase in perceived risk results in a decrease in crystal meth use.

- A substantial majority of 12th graders (over 80 percent) perceive that *regular* use of *any of the illicit drugs* entails a great risk of harm for the user.

- Far fewer 12th graders (just over 50 percent) perceive great risk of harm by experimenting with a drug *once* or *twice*. Although experimenting with drugs is perceived as less risky than regular use, nevertheless a majority of 12th graders believe experimentation with illicit drugs is risky.

WILLINGNESS TO BREAK SOCIAL NORMS AND VIOLATE THE LAW

Social norms about a drug are deeply influenced both by the drug's legal status and whether or not it is considered dangerous. Since methamphetamine use is illegal, except through rare prescriptions, and considered by many to be harmful, its use is discouraged by most of today's American society. Yet, teenagers as a group often rebel against societal norms, and that rebellion often takes the form of drug abuse. It is not surprising that many teens use meth, or at least experiment with it, despite the consequences of clashing with parents, school authorities, and the law. Beyond the high it provides, meth offers teens the means to rebel against authority. Unfortunately, many do not know that the fast-acting addictive qualities of meth make experimentation with it extremely dangerous.

TEEN PERSONALITY AND METH USE

Researchers have long held the hypothesis that drugs cause a teen to behave or act in certain ways. Drug use in adolescence is associated with such traits as poor school performance, delinquency, acts of violence, laziness, and even mental health problems.[16]

However, longitudinal studies on adolescents (studies that track the attitudes and behavior of the same "cohort" [group] of students over a period of time) support a very different hypothesis. Results from these studies have shown

CONVENTIONAL-UNCONVENTIONAL: CAN PERSONALITY PREDICT DRUG USE?[37]

Researchers created a scale of "conventionality-unconventionality" in an attempt to categorize the personality differences between adolescent drug users and nonusers. The basic personality traits of young adolescents were identified prior to their use of any drugs. Based on these personality traits, the adolescents were put into one of two groups: unconventional and conventional. In contrast to the conventional students, the unconventional students showed greater concern for personal independence, a lack of interest in the goals of institutions such as school or church, and a jaundiced view of the larger society around them. Predictions were then made on who would use drugs (unconventional personality) and who would not (conventional personality).

Several years later, the (now) older adolescents were studied again, and the predictive accuracy proved extremely high. The unconventional personality emerged as a key factor in drug experimentation and use among older adolescents. The study indicated that drug use and unconventionality were directly linked: the more unconventional the youth, the greater the likelihood there was of drug experimentation. In addition, the study indicated that the more unconventional the adolescent, the greater the chance there was of having a more serious drug involvement.

that teens who use drugs on a regular basis tend to already have fundamental psychological and behavioral problems. For example, recent research shows that regular illicit drug users, when compared with their peers, performed poorly in high school *before* they started using these drugs. Overall, although regular use of meth may add to a teen's problems, this latter viewpoint suggests that meth use may be more of a symptom than a cause of psychological and behavior problems. Indeed, it is suggested that if meth were not available, a teen with these types of problems would find something else to take its place.[16]

PEER INFLUENCE AND THE DISAPPROVAL FACTOR

Peer influence appears to be one of the strongest factors affecting a teen's decision to use meth and other drugs. In fact, researchers describe the influence of friends as "formidable" when referring to drug-taking decision-making processes. Surveys consistently show that if teens have friends who use drugs, they are more likely to use drugs themselves. Those who do not have friends who use drugs are less likely to use them. Many studies of teenagers report that there is no "forcible" peer pressure involved in the decision to take drugs.[37]

Research also finds that teens taking meth tend to move toward new circles of friends who also use drugs, simultaneously increasing peer acceptance, access to these types of drugs, and the influence of other methamphetamine-using friends. Researchers emphasize that teenagers, particularly older ones, tend to associate with one another on the basis of similarities in lifestyle, values, and behavior. Drug use or nonuse has been determined to be one of those similarities, further enforcing the bond between friends who use or do not use drugs. In this way, teens often "self-select" and choose their friends based upon whether or not they use drugs; this selection process may be the "single most powerful factor" related to drug use among adolescents.[14, 16, 19, 34]

In 2005, MTF survey results showed[19, 34]

- The vast majority of high school seniors (between 82 and 97 percent) do not approve of the regular use of any illicit drugs.

- A majority of 12th graders have friendship circles that do not condone the use of illicit drugs other than marijuana. Well over half (61 percent) believe that their friends would disapprove of their even trying marijuana.

- Paradoxically, 77 percent of 12th graders in 2005 said that their friends use an illicit drug. Researchers believe this means that teens are exposed to many illicit drugs in school.

- According to the 2006 Center on Addiction and Substance Abuse (CASA) survey on teen attitudes about drugs, more than half (51 percent) of high school students say they attend a school where drugs are used, kept, or sold. These results are an improvement from the 2004 survey, where 62 percent of high school students attended a "drug-infected" school.[38]

- Teen risk of drug abuse is 60 percent greater among high school students who say drugs are in their schools.[38]

PARENTAL INFLUENCE

Research shows that parents influence a teen's decision-making process regarding drug use but fail to create or enforce family guidelines about drug use. In addition, a CASA survey revealed that "hands-on" parents who have established rules and expectations for their teens' behavior are more likely to have an "excellent" relationship with their adolescent than "hands-off" parents, and that these involved parents are more likely to live with a teen at less risk of using drugs.[39] For example, parents who establish curfews, expect their teens to respect these curfews, and enforce consequences if curfews are not respected are considered to be "hands-on" parents. As a result, the National Youth Anti-Drug Media Campaign, co-supported by Partnership for a Drug Free America, is aimed more at parents than adolescents, and invites parents to supervise and guide their teen rather than avoid the subject of drug use.[14, 39]

7

Addiction and Recovery

Less than half an hour after I smoked the dope, it kicked in. I had more energy than ever before. My life was suddenly perfect, and I was perfect. I didn't want it to end. I stayed up for seven days. Every half an hour, we'd smoke more to keep up the high. I didn't eat (the dope made food taste like cardboard). Occasionally, someone would drop me off at my house so I could shower and change. My dad freaked out when he saw me. I was enjoying myself too much to care.

Soon I was snorting dope every day. My grades dropped from Bs and Cs to Fs, then I stopped going to school altogether. I eventually got kicked out, but I didn't care. My parents, however, were really upset. My dad and I never used to fight; now all we did was scream at each other. It was the first time I'd ever seen my dad cry.

In December 2004, I got arrested—not for being high (which I was), but for shoplifting at Wal-Mart. That's when my dad told the authorities I needed help. The judge sentenced me to 50 days at a treatment facility.

In rehab, I learned how to deal with my problems. I was really angry before I started using, and meth only made it worse. But I discovered I have a lot of potential, and I don't need meth anymore. My parents and counselor told me they had faith in me to be strong. Four days after returning home, I ran into some friends who asked if I wanted to get high. I was proud of myself for saying no. I get tempted, but now I say, "It's not for me."

—H.P., 16, Easley, South Carolina[1]

WHAT IS METH ADDICTION?

Drug addiction is characterized as a compulsive craving for a drug, a need for ever-increasing quantities of that drug, withdrawal symptoms if a drug is not used regularly, and continuation of drug use regardless of negative circumstances or consequences. Addiction is referred to as a disease.[16]

The word addiction comes from the Latin *addicere*, meaning "to give oneself up." Meth addicts cannot say no to taking the drug, even when they recognize there are negative consequences to continuing the drug, such as failing school, losing the trust and respect of a parent or best friend, having a criminal record, or becoming anorexic or chronically sick. For example, cigarette smokers who have chronic bronchitis, yet continue to smoke, are addicted to tobacco. Addicts are usually in denial to the extent of their drug abuse, and often are blinded to the risks and consequences of using meth even when everyone around them can see its destructive force.[27]

An important characteristic of addiction is tolerance—a frequent need for ever-increasing quantities of meth to maintain the same effects as when the drug use first began. Another defining trait of addiction is having withdrawal symptoms, including cravings. Cravings are a daily symptom of meth addiction because, as discussed, the brain soon craves the drug to supply it with dopamine. These brain cravings cause the meth addict to feel extremely uncomfortable, agitated, unhappy, and hopeless until the next meth high is experienced. Cravings cause the meth addict to have an intense preoccupation with getting and using meth at the expense of any other activity such as school, jobs, friendships, and personal hygiene.[27]

Withdrawal from meth produces the opposite of its stimulating effects. This compounds the unpleasant feelings associated with cravings. Stimulation, strength, and alertness become sluggishness, fatigue, and apathy. Focus and euphoria become disorientation and extreme depression. Without meth, the addict is voraciously hungry, falls into a coma-like sleep, and experiences chills, tremors, and muscle pains.[2, 7, 9]

These physical effects that result from tolerance, cravings, and withdrawal in the body are caused by changes in a meth abuser's brain chemistry, and are the hallmark of drug addiction.

METH ADDICTION ON THE RISE?

In the last 15 years, meth use and abuse has spread to all areas of the country. Even though teen meth use has decreased over the past few years, the overall number of people of all ages who use meth keeps rising each year.

One of the most reliable indicators for measuring this increase in meth abuse is data collected on those admitted to national drug treatment programs for meth addiction.[11] This information is analyzed by the Drug and Alcohol Services Information System (DASIS) and is called the Treatment Episode Data Set (TEDS).[40] These programs operate under the Substance Abuse and Mental Health Services Administration, the same group that runs the National Surveys on Drug Use and Health (NSDUH).

The 2004 TEDS report (the most recent data) provides a variety of information about the 1.9 million people who checked in for drug addiction treatment in 2004. Demographics, including geographic location, age, and gender, along with the types of drugs mentioned as the primary source of the addiction, are examples of the data collected. Most drug users are multiple drug users, so they are asked about the primary drug for which they are seeking addiction treatment.[40]

Teens can enter a drug rehabilitation program in a variety of ways. A teen can "self-refer" on his or her own behalf. Or, a teen can enter a program via intervention by parents, a school, social service agency, temple or church, substance abuse or health care provider, or the criminal justice system.[40]

Data collected from TEDS indicates that the criminal justice system refers the greatest number of people to substance abuse treatment facilities. Justice system referrals, as defined by TEDS, include any referral from a police official, judge, prosecutor, probation officer, or other person affiliated with the judicial system. They also include court referrals for driving under the influence of drugs as well as referrals to treatment in lieu of prosecution of a drug offense.

TEDS reports that between 1993 and 2003, the criminal justice system admitted more 12- to 17-year-olds to treatment programs than any other age group or any other route of referral to drug treatment programs (52 percent in 2003 versus 38 percent in 1993). It is unclear whether this means more teen meth abusers needed treatment or if heightened focus on meth resulted in increased arrests.[40]

TEDS data from the past 15 years illustrate the spread of meth across the United States. The data show both an increase in admissions for meth as well as an increase in the number of states with meth admissions. Methamphetamine and amphetamines are grouped as stimulants in the data.[40]

- In 2004, five drugs made up the overwhelming percentage (95 percent) of all TEDS admissions. These drugs were alcohol (40 percent), opiates (18 percent; primarily heroin), marijuana/hashish (16 percent), cocaine (14 percent), and stimulants (8 percent).

- The proportion of admissions (all ages) for methamphetamine/amphetamine abuse increased from 3 percent to 8 percent between 1994 and 2004.

- Methamphetamine makes up the majority of stimulant admissions for treatment of addiction (86 percent).

- Although in recent years the actual number of teen meth users has decreased, the percentage of youth (12- to 17-year-olds) *admitted for stimulant addiction* rose from 6 to 9 percent between 1993 and 2003. This piece of information is one of the main reasons why communities and lawmakers are saying that meth use is an urgent and pressing issue.

- The increasing numbers of meth abuse admissions in every state in the country illustrates the spread of meth across the nation. Between 1993 and 2003, methamphetamine/amphetamine abuse admissions increased from 13 admissions out of 100,000 admissions to 56 per 100,000 of those aged 12 or older.

- In 2003, 18 states far exceeded the national average of methamphetamine/amphetamine admissions. Ten of these states were in the West, six in the Midwest, and two were in the South. None were in the Northeast. This data pinpoints the intensity of meth use and its geographic spread across the country.

TEENS AT RISK OF ABUSING METHAMPHETAMINE

Teenagers at risk for developing an abusive relationship with methamphetamine can include those who:

- Live with family conflict and discord. Adolescents whose parents are often in conflict, frequently absent, or inconsistent in setting boundaries and guidance are more likely to use illegal drugs. Teens may use meth to cope with family stress, low self-esteem, depression, anger, and anxiety.[39]

- Do not fit in with peers. Some adolescents, particularly those girls who physically mature sooner than others, may feel out of place. Cognitive differences—from those teens with attention deficit syndrome to those with extraordinary intelligence—can put some distance between students and their contemporaries. Those excluded from the mainstream may find that drug use means ready acceptance among a cluster of new friends.[39]

- Want to lose weight. Teen girls are especially susceptible to using meth as they are confronted with unrealistically thin body images (often supported by television and Hollywood). The addictive brain cravings can lead a teen unwittingly into anorexia.[1]

- Are bored or have witnessed the sale of drugs in their neighborhood or school.[38]

- Associate with drug-using friends. As discussed earlier, peer influence is one of the strongest factors in predicting meth use among teens.[16, 39]

REINFORCEMENT: THE KEY MOTIVATOR

Positive reinforcement occurs when a teen receives a pleasurable sensation from using meth and is motivated to use methamphetamine again to achieve the same pleasurable experience. The intensity of the pleasure that a drug delivers to the user is also a reinforcer of the experience. The more the drug experience is pleasurable, the more the user's experience is reinforcing, and therefore the higher the drug's potential for addiction.[34]

Negative experiences are equally as reinforcing as good drug-taking experiences. Some teens experience meth's effects as unpleasant. Although many love the roller coaster highs of meth, others do not, and find meth's racing heart, anxiety, and jitteriness so uncomfortable that they never use it again.[16]

Those teens that enjoy meth's roller coaster ride also quickly understand that the aftereffects of meth's lows are as intense as meth's euphoric highs. Coming down from a meth high can be a very negative experience, replete with depression, fatigue, digestive problems, and body pain. This reinforces the drug-taking behavior, as meth users take more meth to escape these negative experiences.[7, 9]

Achieving pleasant or euphoric moods is clearly a perceived effect of methamphetamine use. But it is equally important to recognize that avoiding unpleasant moods or situations can be another important motivator, and therefore is another dimension of reinforcement. Both experiences—pleasure or avoidance of pain or sadness—can lead the teen meth user toward addiction. In fact, researchers believe that teens who use meth to seek relief from emotional pains such as anger, depression, or family/school problems are experiencing even stronger reinforcement for repeated meth use than those motivated by a desire for euphoria.[16]

Certain routes of exposure to a drug are more reinforcing than others. Because smoking and injecting meth produces a high within seconds, its pleasurable effects are more reinforcing than eating or snorting the drug.

PREVENTING METH USE: WHAT WORKS, WHAT DOESN'T

Prevention of drug abuse is easier, more cost-effective, and preferable to treatment for drug abuse. The earlier a possible drug dependency or strong probability of drug use is identified, the better the chance of correcting it. For example, by

ADDICTION: A STRANGE SORT OF MAGIC

In the book *From Chocolate to Morphine*, researchers Andrew Weil, M.D., and Winifred Rosen commented on the fundamental nature of addiction, writing: "Addiction is a basic human problem whose roots go very deep. Most of us have at some point been wounded, no matter what kind of family we grew up in. We long for a sense of completeness and wholeness, and most often search for satisfaction outside of ourselves. Ironically, whatever satisfaction we gain from drugs, food, money and other 'sources' of pleasure really comes from inside of us. That is, we project our power onto external substances and activities, allowing them to make us feel better temporarily. This is a very strange sort of magic. We give away our power in exchange for a transient sense of wholeness, then suffer because the objects of our craving seem to control us. Addiction can be cured only when we consciously experience this process, reclaim our power, and recognize that our wounds must be healed from within."[16]

understanding the predictive factors of teen meth use, young children can be identified as "at risk" for use of drugs prior to using drugs. Informing these potential young users about the negative effects and risks of meth use (or any drug), as well as exploring drug alternatives, may be an effective prevention tool.

Current U.S. antidrug education and prevention campaigns increased in reach and frequency in the 1980s. Since then, adolescents have seen antidrug messages virtually everywhere—on shopping bags, comic books, restaurant place mats, billboards, television, bumper stickers, and candy wrappers. Beginning in elementary school, the D.A.R.E. (Drug Abuse Resistance Education) program sends uniformed police officers into schools to teach about the dangers of drugs. Researchers tell us that today's teenagers have had more drug education than any group of young people in American history.[16]

There is little scientific evidence to support the effectiveness of antidrug messages or their impact on the drug-use decisions of adolescents.[41] Media campaigns such as the *Partnership for a Drug-Free America* have strengthened antidrug attitudes and behaviors among young children and non-drug-using adults, but not in teenagers. Several recent studies report similar findings about the D.A.R.E. program.[41]

ZERO TOLERANCE

The concept of "zero tolerance" drives much of today's legal and educational policy. The zero tolerance policies teach that using a drug such as meth even *once* puts the user at risk for abuse and addiction. Most American drug education programs are built around this zero tolerance message. This policy stresses that the purpose of drug education is to prevent drug experimentation; therefore, the topic of drug *use* is practically forbidden.

This presents a dilemma. The zero tolerance approach contradicts the natural propensity of teens to want to learn about and possibly experiment with illegal drugs.

Figure 7.1 Community programs like D.A.R.E. strive to prevent children and teenagers from experimenting with or abusing drugs. © William Campbell/Sygma/CORBIS

Additionally, most school-based drug education classes fail to provide information on the relative risks of different drugs, doses, routes of exposure, or patterns of use—the very basics of drug education.

As part of the zero tolerance policy, most schools impose harsh sanctions, including expulsion from school, for any use or possession of meth. Many students are reluctant to discuss their own drug use in drug education classrooms out of fear of these strict sanctions. Most drug education programs in American schools today do not seem to provide effective drug education for teenagers.[16]

In the 1970s, the National Institute on Drug Abuse endorsed an alternative approach to drug education. This approach, devised by researchers, psychologists, and drug-policy analysts, declared that the goal of drug education was to reduce drug *abuse*, not *use*. The proponents of this new policy argued that moralizing about drugs was ineffective, exaggerating the dangers from drugs was counterproductive (and might even lead more youth to try drugs), and expecting adolescents to be totally abstinent was unrealistic.[7]

Although this prevention approach was incorporated into some educational materials for a short time, it was abandoned in the early 1980s during President Ronald Reagan's campaign of "Just Say No" to drugs. Since then, zero tolerance has been the predominant educational antidrug approach in American classrooms.

HARM REDUCTION

Based on evidence that "Just Say No" does not seem to discourage teens from using drugs, many experts point out the success of "harm reduction" models of drug education. Proponents of harm reduction do not encourage or condone drug use, but

Figure 7.2 Rallies and community programs are part of the "Just Say No" campaign aimed at helping children avoid drug abuse. © Patrick Bennett/CORBIS

they assume that many adolescents will eventually experiment with illicit drugs. Since their goal is to lessen the harms associated with drug use, these programs actively educate adolescents about the relative risks of drugs and their responsible use. Most harm reduction education targets teenagers, since they are the age group most likely to experiment with drugs.[16]

Harm reduction is very controversial. Opponents believe it condones drug use, and may lull teens into thinking drugs are safe. Proponents think it can save lives. In an interesting comparison of zero tolerance versus harm reduction policies, statistics show that 34 percent of those over the age of 15 in the United States (with a zero tolerance policy) have used the illicit drug marijuana at least once, as compared to only 19 percent of 15-year-olds in the Netherlands (which has a harm reduction policy).[42] While it is possible that other factors affect these use patterns, there appears to be evidence that harm reduction does not lead to increased drug use.

TREATING METH ADDICTION

Two basic forms of meth addiction treatment are available: inpatient and outpatient. Inpatient (residential) treatment involves an extensive stay in a hospital or residential treatment center. Most common are 30- to 90-day programs, but meth addicts often need to stay at a center for a year or longer. This length of time gives the brain's damaged dopamine neurons a chance to repair themselves; the meth addict needs this time to deal with and heal the corresponding physical and psychological effects that result from this brain damage. Although recovery is possible, relapse to meth addiction is a possibility even after successful treatment. Intensive outpatient support is needed for a year or longer after this inpatient phase.[27]

Treatment for meth dependence begins with a user's own recognition that he or she is dependent and that this dependency is a problem in his or her life. Many successful recovery groups such as Narcotics Anonymous have the philosophy that effective drug treatment is entirely dependent on an individual's motivation to change.[27]

Individuals who seek treatment assistance under pressure, against their will, or who are not motivated to take responsibility for their drug-taking choices are not likely to have successful treatment outcomes. However, treatment does not need to be voluntary to be effective. Sometimes strong motivation can assist the treatment process. **Interventions** with family and friends, punishments or enticements by the family or school, or potential criminal penalties can significantly impact the decision of a meth user to seek and stay in treatment.[16]

The majority of drug treatment programs are designed to help manage the effects of psychological dependence.[27] This is good for meth addicts because the psychological effects of meth withdrawal are very powerful and can be difficult to overcome. Traditional drug treatment programs may include individual, group, and/or family counseling in conjunction with 12-step programs (such as Narcotics Anonymous).

One form of outpatient treatment is known as the Matrix, created during the 1980s by the Matrix Institute on Addictions group in Southern California, with funding from NIDA. The multielement approach of the Matrix includes cognitive behavioral therapies (such as relapse prevention techniques), positive-reinforcing treatment, family involvement, psychoeducational information, 12-step efforts, and regular urine testing. Outpatients participate in group and individual sessions several times a week for four months, followed by eight months of continuing care support and 12-step program participation. To date, more than 15,000 meth and cocaine users have participated in the program.[43]

In 1999, UCLA coordinated a large-scale evaluation of the Matrix Model, with funding from the Center for Substance Abuse Treatment, for the treatment of meth users. Approximately 1,000 meth-dependent individuals were admitted into eight different treatment study sites. In each of the sites, 50 percent of the participants were randomly assigned to either

the Matrix treatment or to a "treatment as usual" (TAU) condition (consisting of a variety of counseling techniques). The
study results showed that individuals assigned to the Matrix
approach treatment received substantially more treatment
services, stayed in treatment longer, gave more meth-negative
urine samples during treatment, and completed treatment
at a higher rate than those in the TAU condition. When data
at discharge and follow-up were examined, it appeared that
both treatment conditions produced similar outcomes. Participants in both conditions showed very significant reductions in meth use, significant improvements in psychosocial
functioning, and substantial reductions in psychological
symptoms, including depression. Post-treatment data showed
that over 60 percent of both treatment groups reported no
meth use and gave urine samples that tested negative for
meth (and cocaine) use. Use of alcohol, marijuana, and other
drugs was also significantly reduced.[43]

An overall goal of treatment programs is to help dependent
drug users identify and understand the motivators that drive
their drug use. Together, the recovering drug abuser and the
team at the treatment center can devise healthier, nondrug-
taking ways to cope. Effective drug treatment programs for
teens are geared exclusively to their age group. Being with
adolescents who share the same problem is likely to be
therapeutic for those who may feel isolated from their peers.

The National Association of State Alcohol and Drug Abuse
Directors reported that "clinically appropriate treatment provided by qualified and trained staff is effective in stopping
methamphetamine use," in its 2005 "Fact Sheet: Methamphetamine." To further support this statement, they provided the
following examples of treatment success in specific states:

- **Colorado**: 80 percent of meth users were abstinent at
  time of discharge from treatment

- **Tennesee**: 65 percent were abstinent six months after
  discharge

- **Texas:** 88 percent were abstinent 60 days after discharge

- **Utah:** 60.8 percent were abstinent at time of discharge[44]

In 2004, Iowa had reported similar success with its publicly funded substance abuse treatment programs, with 65.5 percent of Iowan methamphetamine clients still abstinent six months after being discharged from treatment.[45]

Meth addicts tend to suffer from depression, low energy, and anhedonia (no feelings of pleasure), as well as experience extreme paranoia and hallucinations.[9] These feelings are extremely uncomfortable and can last for many months. Recovering meth addicts can feel suicidal because of these effects, and many meth abusers go back to the drug as a result. Many treatment programs now prescribe antidepressant and antipsychotic drugs to offset these effects, in addition to psychotherapy. In some recovering meth addicts, these withdrawal symptoms never totally go away. They may need to take these antidepressant and antipsychotic drugs for the rest of their lives.[9, 11]

REDUCING CRAVINGS

A major goal in treating meth addiction is the reduction of cravings for meth. These cravings plague the meth abuser who is trying to clean the drug from his or her body and are a common reason for relapse. So far there is no prescription drug to alleviate meth cravings in the treatment process, but studies on the antidepressant drug bupropion show preliminary success in reducing meth cravings as well as the psychological hardship that defines meth withdrawal.[46]

Other drug rehabilitation programs assert that cravings result from a depletion of the meth abuser's bodily defenses. They use more alternative forms of treatment to stop cravings, giving heavy doses of vitamins, minerals, and neurotransmitters to meth abusers to help replenish what was lost during their time using the drug. These programs report a successful reduction in cravings that make it easier for a recovering meth addict to stick with the counseling part of the treatment program.[47]

The ancient practice of ear **acupuncture** is also used with success at alleviating the discomforting effects of drug withdrawal. Five sliver-thin needles are inserted into ear points thought to regulate the nervous system, cerebral cortex, respiratory system, liver, and kidneys. The U.S. government has granted millions of dollars to study this promising drug treatment method.[47]

WILD DRUG ABUSE TREATMENT

Although drug dependency often masks other mental health problems, these core issues cannot be addressed until a meth-abuser becomes sober. Some meth-dependent teens go to treatment centers because they have grown desperate and asked their parents for help; sometimes parents force their addicted teen into a treatment center after seeing the unraveling of their child's life because of meth use.

Therapeutic boarding schools are facilities that rely on a wilderness-survival approach. Using nature, a skilled staff, vigorous exercise, and **group therapy**, these programs can run for two months or more and take place in wilderness areas mainly in the West. They nurture self-reliance and self-respect as teens come to terms with their behavior problems while backpacking, surviving, and thriving in nature. Counselors say adolescents in modern society do not go through the traditional rites of passage that came with growing up and crossing into adulthood. Instead of hunting for food, taking care of younger siblings, and learning to build shelter, for example, young people today often turn to drugs as a way to prove that they are "all grown up." These wilderness programs provide this rite of passage, and have been hailed as lifesavers by some, while others have criticized these programs as being overly strict as well as expensive.[10]

REQUIRED: A SET OF SUPPORTIVE FRIENDS

Once a teen meth abuser clears meth from his or her body and passes through any withdrawal symptoms, the journey to recovery begins. This is not an easy journey. It requires a complete reorganization and restructuring of thought processes, attitudes, and lifestyle. A meth-dependent teen may have organized nearly all daily thoughts and routines around obtaining or using meth. A new direction is needed toward school, work, hobbies, family, religion, and friends—and having fun! Recovery involves a conscious and deliberate effort to create different, more socially productive ways of spending time in order to focus on activities other than using meth.

In essence, recovering teens must entirely change their social structure. One of the hardest things for a teen to do is to stop associating with drug-taking friends. As we have seen, peer influence is one of the strongest predictive factors of teen meth use. Conversely, it is also the most effective deterrent to meth use. Simply put, teens that do not approve of drugs are less likely to use drugs, by themselves, or with their friends.[16, 48]

Treatment programs of varying intensity exist, but all programs have the same fundamental mission: A meth-dependent person must maintain complete abstinence while learning to cope with the emotional and behavioral motivators associated with its abuse. While most of the feelings or motivations for using meth may still exist, a great challenge for the recovering teen is to explore alternative ways of dealing with and expressing those intense feelings.[1, 27]

SOBRIETY HIGH

Sobriety High is a charter high school in Minnesota where recovering teens can stay away from drugs by removing themselves from their old social network. Students can choose to attend these schools or in some cases a court has ordered them to attend. Teens sometimes opt for Sobriety High after "graduating" from a drug treatment facility. In addition to typical required high school classes, students at Sobriety High meet in group therapy as a mandatory class and receive a grade for it. In these sessions, teens discuss their struggles and progress in staying clean. If a student relapses at Sobriety High and tells a staff member, chances are the teen will be allowed to stay. Repeated drug use will get a teen kicked out. For teens using drugs for years, it can be daunting to imagine a life without drugs, but Sobriety High has a wide diversity of classes, extra-curricular activities, and students, all of which make sobriety anything but boring.[10]

HALTING RELAPSE

Relapse is a frequent event in the treatment of addiction. Triggers for relapse include feeling Hungry, Angry, Lonely, and Tired. The acronym HALT is used to help addicted people recognize these common danger signs in their own feelings. Recovering addicts learn that these feelings can often trigger a relapse to meth abuse, and learn how to manage these and other high-risk feelings. **Cognitive behavior therapy** is another powerful tool that can prevent relapse. Therapists use techniques to help recovering meth abusers learn new ways of thinking and behaving so they are able to cope with high-risk situations that might arise in relationships or with certain feelings that might trigger a relapse.[27]

RECOVERY

In many ways, the recovery process is similar to dealing with the loss of a loved one. Recovering teens may need to grieve for the loss of their past history as they move into a new, drug-free life. During such periods of bereavement, teens can experience feelings of depression and emptiness as families, friends, and familiar locations elicit memories of past drug use. Looking back, recovering teens can see how this bereavement period is a natural part of change and growth, and is considered by many to be a healthy sign of a teen maturing to adulthood.[16]

8

Methamphetamine and the Law

The first time I did meth was two summers ago, before a country-music festival. Then I started doing it every day. The first few months, I would get really high and loved it. Then you build up a tolerance, and it never feels the same. I was constantly chasing that early high.

I was getting skinnier, and I loved that. I like to eat and I'm lazy. Meth was a fast way to lose weight. I lost my appetite; food just doesn't taste good when you're on meth. People asked, "What are you doing?" and I was like, "Oh, I'm watching what I eat." My parents noticed, especially my mom. She had to buy me new clothes because nothing fit me. I went from 152 to just 112 pounds, and from a size 13 to a size 2. My face looked sunken, and I had dark circles under my eyes.

I moved in with my boyfriend, and I wanted to do meth all the time. I smoked, snorted, and ate it. Sometimes it made me throw up. I was arrested and charged with theft for (allegedly) stealing a ring. I was in jail for several days. I cried the whole time. My parents said the only way they'd get me out of jail was if I went to rehab. So I went. I was there for six weeks, and I met so many great people. The withdrawal was hard because there's nothing to help you through it. I couldn't sleep, and the meth cravings were really bad. But talking about it in therapy helped. It's awesome to work on myself and finally find out who I am.

—J.S., 21, Peachtree City, Georgia[1]

Methamphetamine without a prescription is illegal to use, possess, manufacture, or distribute. Although the number of people of all ages trying meth in their lifetime is on the rise, teen meth use has been on the decline in the past few years. In comparison to marijuana, cigarettes, alcohol, and cocaine, the numbers of Americans who use meth is quite low.[19, 34, 35, 49] Yet, the irreversible effects from meth addiction, the destruction of property and lives in meth explosions, and the rising number of meth addicts who are incarcerated has captured the attention of the nation's public.

The controversial "war on drugs" has been ongoing in the United States for more than 36 years. Its success is hotly debated. Since its inception, local, state, and federal governments have attempted to control and reduce teen drug use through a variety of legal policies and procedures. Yet despite these efforts, and harsh legal consequences, including jail time and heavy monetary fines, teens and adults continue to make, use, and/or deal methamphetamine.

CURRENT U.S. DRUG POLICY: SUPPLY AND DEMAND

Does the supply and availability of meth drive demand for the drug, or does the demand for meth create willing suppliers, eager to capture their share of the very profitable illegal drug market? The ability to make meth from ordinary, cheap, and easy-to-purchase products is a major reason that meth is such a lucrative, illegal enterprise, and drives the incentive to supply the drug. The stimulating effects and addictive cravings for meth drive demand.

Current U.S. drug policy attempts to reduce both sides of this supply and demand equation. The 2007 budget for the National Drug Control Strategy, as requested by President George W. Bush, supports three key priorities. The first two aim to decrease demand for drugs, incuding meth, and the third focuses on curtailing supply. Priority I is intended to prevent drug use before it starts. Educational and community programs are designed to encourage young people to reject using drugs. Priority II is designed to heal the country's drug abusers and addicts by ensuring that treatment is accessible to all who need it. Priority III seeks to disrupt the drug market by targeting individuals and organizations that profit from illegal drug trafficking.[50]

The drug budget has consistently increased over the past four years. The requested budget for 2007 is $12.7 billion. The budget for 2004 was $12.1 billion; for 2005 it was $12.2 billion; and for 2006 it is $12.5 billion.[50]

There are specific programs that focus on meth in the budget's programs. One program continues the scientific work of the Methamphetamine Clinical Trials Group, which conducts clinical trials of promising medications to treat meth addiction. Another is called COPS, or Community-Oriented Policing Services. This program gives state and local police funding to assist with cleaning up meth labs. The President also increased the budget for the multicultural National Youth Anti-Drug Media Campaign to continue its antidrug message aimed at youth and their parents.[41, 50]

Budgets have also been increased for supply-reduction programs such as the U.S. Drug Enforcement Agency's (DEA) Drug Flow Prevention program, designed to disrupt the flow of drugs, money, and chemicals used by major drug trafficking organizations to manufacture and sell meth and other drugs. Enhanced patrols along trafficking routes to the United States and expanded security forces along U.S. borders (mainly in the Southwest) are also included in the budget.[50]

Enforcing drug trafficking laws in the United States is extremely challenging. According to the U.S. Customs Service, each year 60 million people enter the United States on more than 675,000 commercial and private flights. Another 6 million arrive by sea and 370 million by land. More than 90,000 merchant and passenger ships dock at U.S. ports carrying more than 9 million shipping containers and 400 million tons of cargo. In addition, 116 million vehicles cross the U.S. borders from Canada and Mexico. In the midst of this enormous influx, traffickers conceal drug shipments that are later distributed throughout the United States. Pseudoephedrine, for

Figure 8.1 U.S. Border Patrol agents patrol a road that runs along the international border with Mexico east of Columbus, New Mexico. Large quantities of methamphetamine and other illegal drugs are produced in Mexico and then smuggled across the border for sale in the United States. © Leslie Hoffman/AP Images

example, has been smuggled into the United States by couriers via commercial airlines or tractor-trailers crossing the borders from Canada.[11]

METH: A SCHEDULE II CONTROLLED SUBSTANCE

The mission of the Drug Enforcement Administration, a division of the federal government, is to enforce the drug laws of the United States. The DEA is a principal force in reducing the supply, and therefore the availability, of methamphetamine and other drugs. The DEA was established in 1973 under the U.S. Department of Justice and is responsible for enforcing the guidelines of the Controlled Substances Act of 1970.[23]

This act provides the legal foundation for today's national drug policy. It places "controlled substances"—drugs that are regulated under existing federal law—into one of five schedules. Scheduled drugs are categorized by their distinguishing chemical properties, including their potential for abuse and their medical usefulness. Schedule 1 categorizes the most dangerous drugs that have no recognized medical use, while Schedule V classifies the least dangerous drugs as a group.

In legal terms, any use, possession, manufacture, or distribution of the substances controlled in Schedules I through V of the Controlled Substances Act is considered drug abuse and is subject to state and federal penalties.[23]

Under the Controlled Substances Act, meth is categorized as a Schedule II drug (along with amphetamines, cocaine, and morphine). Schedule II drugs are defined as: 1) drugs with a high potential for abuse, 2) drugs that, when abused, may lead to severe psychological or physical dependence, and 3) drugs that have an accepted medical use with severe restrictions. These drugs are only available legally with a prescription, and are closely monitored by the DEA.[11]

A LEGAL HISTORY OF CUTTING OFF SUPPLY

Federal and state officials have enacted laws since 1970 to target three main areas of meth manufacture: regulation and restriction of precursor chemicals and equipment used to make meth, finding and shutting down illegal labs, and breaking up the organized drug syndicates that manufacture and distribute meth.[12]

POSSESSION AND THE LAW

People found with illegal drugs on their person (or in their cars or houses) are considered guilty of possession. The consequences of a possession charge depend on the drug, the quantity of drug, and the state in which the person is arrested. In many states, merely being in the company of someone who is in possession of illegal drugs (even if you are unaware of that situation) can make you guilty of possession.

With the passage of the Controlled Substances Act in 1970, lawmakers classified injectable methamphetamine as a Schedule II drug, recognizing its potential for abuse.[5] Critics of the illegalization of drugs point out that once a drug is made illegal, its production does not cease, but instead goes underground and becomes an increasingly profitable criminal enterprise. It can be seen as a type of evolutionary process. A lull in meth-making activity comes immediately after a new regulation goes into effect. Ever-adaptable meth manufacturers have, to date, always found ways around new laws, and eventually start production again with a few modifications. Law enforcement is in the difficult position of constantly chasing a moving target.

In the 1970s and 1980s, West coast biker gangs illicitly produced meth using a method known as P2P (the chemical precursor was phenyl-2-propanone.) In 1980, government officials regulated P2P as an illegal substance. It became very difficult to acquire P2P, and meth production and use went down. This decline was not due to a decrease in demand but rather a decrease in supply.[2]

Biker meth cooks discovered that ephedrine, found in Sudafed and other over-the-counter cold medicines, produced a type of meth that was more potent than the meth made from P2P. They also discovered that pseudoephedrine could serve as a precursor chemical.[11]

The Controlled Substances Act was amended to restrict these and other chemical precursors through the Chemical Diversion and Trafficking Act of 1988, under which 12 precursor chemicals became strictly regulated by the DEA. These chemicals are known as "Listed Chemicals." Today, over 35 chemicals are listed and regulated by the DEA.[23]

List 1 Chemicals are precursors such as ephedrine and pseudoephedrine that can be directly converted to an illicit drug. List 2 Chemicals are used in the manufacture of illegal drugs, such as iodine, red phosphorus, and hydrochloric acid.

Figure 8.2 A Pierce County sheriff's deputy places a suspect under arrest for having a portable methamphetamine lab in the trunk of a stolen car he possessed near Tacoma, Washington. © Lui Kit Wong/AP Images

These three chemicals are used to make hydriodic acid, a key ingredient that extracts ephedrine from cold medicines in order to produce methamphetamine.[23, 41, 51]

The Controlled Substances Act required suppliers of these listed chemicals to keep records of import and sales documents. Federal officials hoped the law would curtail the supply of these needed ingredients to make meth, for instance, by tracking unusually large shipments and sales of precursor chemicals.[11, 23] However, some of these chemicals are here for larger, legitimate uses in the chemical and pharmaceutical industry, and diversion is always possible.

THE UNNECESSARY EPIDEMIC AND PHARMACEUTICAL COMPANIES

A senior DEA official involved with drafting the law was aware of the spread of meth at this time, and wanted to set limits on the amount of cold and allergy medicines customers could buy. The $252 billion a year pharmaceutical industry, with its strong, organized, political lobbying power, was able to remove that restriction from the law. In addition, they were able to insert a loophole in the law that exempted legal products, such as a tablet, that already contained ephedrine and pseudoephedrine. This meant that importers of raw ephedrine and pseudoephedrine powder had to keep records, but sellers of finished pills or liquids containing the chemicals did not.[11, 52]

Lack of restrictions to close these loopholes in the pharmaceutical industry during the late 1980s may have directly contributed to an "unnecessary" meth epidemic. There are only nine legal producers of raw ephedrine and pseudoephedrine in the world. Tighter regulations of these huge laboratories could have also reduced the supply of meth in the United States. However, cocaine and heroin were much bigger problems at the time, and meth took a "bureaucratic back seat." Still, the pharmaceutical industry knew their products were being used to make methamphetamine.[11]

STRICTER CONTROLS ON EPHEDRINE

Meth manufacturers managed to exploit legal loopholes in the Chemical Diversion and Trafficking Act. In the early 1990s, meth cooks simply began using pills from cold and allergy medications containing ephedrine and pseudoephedrine since they were unregulated by law.

A Mexican drug cartel run by the Amezcua brothers began buying ephedrine in bulk from some of the overseas producers that also supply the pharmaceutical companies with their legal supplies to make cold medicines. Superlabs appeared in California, producing meth that was twice as potent as before, including crystal meth.[11]

In 1993, the Domestic Chemical Diversion Control Act was enacted and put stricter regulations on ephedrine. Ephedrine was the precursor used in 79 percent of all meth labs seized by the DEA that year, while pseudoephedrine was used in fewer than 2 percent of the seized laboratories.[11, 14]

A U.S. customs agent discovered 3.4 metric tons of ephedrine powder during a routine search on a plane traveling from Switzerland to Mexico in 1994. The chemical was traced to a factory in India that turned out to be the Amezcua cartel's source for several years. The DEA learned that during one 18-month period, the Amezcua traffickers smuggled in 170 tons of ephedrine to the United States. That amount is enough to produce two *billion* hits of meth.[11]

By 1996, pseudoephedrine was identified as the precursor in more than 75 percent of the seized laboratories that year. Once again, meth manufacturers had learned to go with the federal government's flow, and began using pseudoephedrine in their recipes instead of the more regulated ephedrine.[11, 23]

THE COMPREHENSIVE METHAMPHETAMINE CONTROL ACT OF 1996

The Comprehensive Methamphetamine Control Act of 1996 was passed to regulate pseudoephedrine, putting into effect a provision that had been desired 10 years earlier but had been shot down by the pharmaceutical industry. The law put restrictions on legal products containing ephedrine and pseudoephedrine. The DEA reached a compromise with the pharmaceutical industry to accomplish this. Customers were restricted to purchasing three packs of cold medications at a time. Ephedrine-only products (pure ephedrine tablets) were stored behind the counter, and sales were recorded for the DEA. Pharmacists began to train their employees to monitor "suspicious" transactions of individual customers who bought very large amounts of these regulated products.[11]

The law exempted pills sold in blister packs, as the DEA thought it would be too cumbersome for illegal drug manufacturers to use in large volumes. Within three years, blister packs of pseudoephedrine were found in 47 percent of seized meth labs.[11]

Wholesale distributors of over-the-counter cold medicines needed to register with the DEA for a license under this new law. The DEA took a year to put the licensing part of the law into effect. By that time, there was an overflow of wholesalers requesting a license to sell pseudoephedrine since the cartels were using that precursor exclusively. Before long, companies set up as brokers for the meth cartels made millions of dollars by selling pseudoephedrine to the superlabs. Wholesalers licensed by the U.S. government conducted all of this illegal business.[11]

CANADIAN EXPORT OF PSEUDOEPHEDRINE

Over the next few years, the DEA cracked down on "bogus" pseudoephedrine wholesalers, and the meth supply dried up a bit. But this has been part of an unfortunate pattern. Each time the federal government passed a meth law, it only affected a piece of the meth supply problem. After each regulation, the meth supply went down, its purity decreased, and its price increased—for a short while. Each time the meth cooks found new ways to make their product and to supply their waiting customers with meth.

At this time, pseudoephedrine was unregulated in Canada. Over a period of four years, Canada's bulk pseudoephedrine imports for the manufacture of cold pills quadrupled as these raw ingredients actually were diverted to supply meth makers in the United States.[11]

Meanwhile, the federal government attempted to curtail the ways meth cooks obtained their recipes and other meth-making communication channels with the 2000 Meth Anti-Proliferation Act. Civil rights organizations lobbied for cuts to many of the provisions of the original law that actually would have infringed upon the American public's right to free speech. The enacted law further reduced the number of cold/allergy

TRENDS IN METH LAB SEIZURES

Meth lab seizure data shows us the spread of meth across the country, from the Western states to the Midwest to the South. Is the Northeast next? Note the sharp decline in meth lab seizures in the Western states. Is this due to less drug use or to the superlabs moving down to Mexico after tighter regulations were enforced in the United States in 2004 and 2005?[15]

Clandestine Meth Laboratory Incidents* [15]

	1999	2001	2003	2005
Missouri	439	2,180	2,885	2,170
Iowa	352	578	1,272	753
Tennessee	143	495	953	861
Indiana	151	521	979	915
Michigan	10	122	267	341
Oklahoma	404	806	1,068	217
Oregon	264	587	419	189
Nevada	290	259	131	52
Washington	599	1,480	1,011	522
California	2,579	1,883	1,287	468
Arizona	380	312	140	75

Adapted from: National Clandestine Laboratory Database, 1999–2005.[15]

*The majority of seized labs are home labs, not superlabs. Incidents included findings of labs, lab equipment, chemicals, and dumpsites.

medications that could be sold at one time by retailers. These regulations applied to grocery stores, drug stores, pharmacies, mail order, and any other retail distributors of ephedrine or pseudoephedrine products.[41]

In 2003, Canada regulated pseudoephedrine and joined forces with the DEA to crack down on illegal exportation of this precursor. From Steve Suo, investigative reporter for *The Oregonian*:

> "The [Royal] Canadian Mounted Police would pursue these loads of pseudoephedrine from Ontario, follow it all the way up to the border at Detroit and hand off the surveillance to the DEA, which would pick it up and follow it all the way across the country to California, where they in some cases actually were able to pursue the loads up to meth labs and then shut them down." [11]

SUPERLABS MOVE TO MEXICO

The U.S. DEA was becoming bad for business, and the Mexican drug cartels moved south, where pseudoephedrine was unregulated. In 2004, Mexico legally imported 224 tons of pseudoephedrine, an amount that was twice as much needed to make cold medicine. The extra 100 tons was cooked into meth, and smuggled, like other drugs, across the border into the United States. (At least six cartels are known to exist today.) [11]

STOPPING SUPPLY AT THE SOURCE

Superlabs require large amounts of ephedrine or pseudoephedrine, and can produce 100,000 doses of meth, compared to home labs that produce about 300 doses. [11] Because of this need, cartels are reliant on the nine international sources for their supply. DEA authorities believe that the spread of meth can be halted if these precursor chemicals are regulated at their international sources and in the countries that import them. The DEA would like to see that countries import only enough of the chemicals needed to satisfy legitimate national demand for pseudoephedrine and ephedrine-containing cold and cough remedies. [11, 52, 53]

OKLAHOMA PASSES MOST STRINGENT LAW YET

In April 2004, Oklahoma was the first state to enact meth leg-islation. The state classified ephedrine and pseudoephedrine as Schedule V drugs. This meant the medicines containing these chemicals had to be kept behind a pharmacist's counter or in a locked case, and the buyer of this medication had to show photo identification, sign a logsheet, and be over the age of 18. Most important, the sale of these medicines was now extremely limited without a prescription from a doctor. Oklahoma saw an immediate reduction (51 percent) in the number of meth lab seizures between 2004 and 2005. Over the next several years, 35 states passed similar laws.[10, 12]

Other important meth strategies have been unfolding over the past two years. In California, there was a noticeable increase in pseudoephedrine originating from China once the Cana-dian supply diminished. China has one of the world's largest chemical industries. Hong Kong in particular was also a source of pseudoephedrine tablets being diverted to Mexican labs. The United States, Mexico, and China worked out a commit-ment to regulate the shipments, and in November 2005, China passed its first law on precursor chemicals aimed at preventing their illicit use.[12]

Meth's precursors, ephedrine, pseudoephedrine, and chemicals used in its manufacture, including iodine and red phosphorus, were being auctioned through the popular Web site eBay. The DEA and eBay reached an agreement, and eBay no longer allows these products to be auctioned on their site. The DEA expected to reach similar agreements with Google and Yahoo.[12]

THE COMBAT METHAMPHETAMINE EPIDEMIC ACT OF 2006

Passed in March 2006, this federal anti-meth law is the first to address the meth problem from all angles, including precursor control, international controls, environmental regulation, and criminal prosecution. The law fills in many of the loopholes of

Figure 8.3 New laws sharply limit the quantity of over-the-counter drugs containing ephedrine that a customer may purchase at one time. © Darron Cummings/AP Images

prior anti-meth laws, including the blister-pack conundrum that previously allowed unlimited sales of cold medicines in blister packs. Now ephedrine and pseudoephedrine products can be bought only in very limited quantities (two packages), regardless of their packaging. This law is similar to many state laws, requiring medicines that contain pseudoephedrine and ephedrine be stored in locked cabinets, purchasers sign a logbook, etc. It also allows prosecution of meth manufacturers for polluting water and dumping hazardous waste, and requires a convicted meth manufacturer to pay for the cleanup from the lab scene. The DEA designed a new category under the Controlled Substances Act for ephedrine and pseudoephedrine, creating opportunities for more severe penalties of convicted meth traffickers and manufacturers.[41, 54]

The United States and Mexico have formed a partnership to address the production and trafficking of meth. In May

2006, an anti-methamphetamine initiative was announced between the two countries. Among other things, Mexico has placed new import **quotas** on pseudoephedrine and will allow only licensed pharmacies to sell medicines containing pseudoephedrine.[11]

The effectiveness of these measures remains to be seen. After every federal anti-meth regulation has passed, the Mexican cartels have found ways to adapt. Now that Mexico is regulating its pseudoephedrine imports, the cartels may adjust again by moving to other countries in Latin America or by importing finished meth from Asia, where the drug is very popular. Time will tell what effect these new laws have on the supply and demand of meth.[11, 23, 26]

UPDATE ON PHARMACEUTICALS

During the 1990s, the pharmaceutical maker of Sudafed (Pfizer) tried including additives that would make it harder for meth cooks to extract pseudoephedrine. Tests showed that the body had difficulty absorbing the decongestant because of the additives, and the work was abandoned.

Pfizer now has another version of Sudafed on the market called Sudafed PE. It contains the decongestant phenylephrine that cannot be turned into meth. Other companies are beginning to put phenylephrine into their cold remedies, as well as other alternatives that are not meth precursors. However, it is unclear whether these products will be as successful for consumers or meet the pharmaceutical companies' financial goals.

We saw in Chapter Three that the *l*-form of methamphetamine does not have the same effects as the *d*-form. In the same way, there is a possible solution in a "mirror image" form of pseudoephedrine because it cannot be turned into methamphetamine. But product development has not been pursued because getting FDA (Food and Drug Administration) approval would be a long, expensive road for Pfizer. Although Congress has allocated millions of dollars to study the effects

of meth on the brain, and the damage it causes, it has not significantly financed research into a cold remedy that cannot be
turned into meth.[11]

METH PENALTIES

There are three underlying principles that help provide an
understanding of current U.S. drug law. First, the levels of
punishment for a drug violation are based on the amount of
the drug that one possesses or distributes. Second, the penalties
for a second offense are harsher than the penalties for a first
offense. Third, state drug laws differ from each other and from
those established by the federal legal system. (Even though
some states follow the penalty standards set by the federal government, they are not required to do so).[54]

Possession of small amounts of some drugs can be considered a misdemeanor, while possession of larger amounts of
drugs are often considered felonies, depending upon the most
recent definitions of the drug laws and whether the offender
is charged with a state or federal drug law violation. A misdemeanor is a civil offense that might result in a fine, public
service, or a short prison sentence (less than one year). A felony
is a criminal offense; once convicted, felons not only face mas-
sive fines and lengthy prison terms, but also lose the ability to
obtain student and small-business loans, governmental grants
and employment, and even rights of American citizenship as
basic as voting.[54]

The federal penalties for drug trafficking are harsh. A
first offense conviction for the possession, manufacture, or
distribution of five to 49 grams of pure meth (or 50 to 499
grams mixture) carries a five-to-40-year jail sentence along
with a fine of up to $2 million. A *second offense* conviction for
the same amount of meth carries a 10-year-to-life jail sentence,
and a fine of up to $4 million. These penalties increase if
even larger quantities of meth are involved. In addition,
the new anti-meth law passed this year makes the penalties
even tougher. Cooking or dealing methamphetamine in the

presence of children raises the federal penalty by up to 20 additional years in prison.[54]

The new law also increases federal penalties for retail and wholesale distributors of any medicines containing the chemical precursors or equipment and chemicals that can be used in a meth lab. Any person who knowingly and "recklessly" exceeds the sales limit, does not require identification, does not use a log book, or fails to follow any of the other regulations is *guilty of a first offense*, which includes up to a $25,000 fine and up to a year in prison. Penalties increase with repeated offenses.[54]

In Canada, the maximum penalty for production and distribution of methamphetamine has increased from 10 years to life in prison.[54]

METH AND THE JUVENILE JUSTICE SYSTEM

The first juvenile court in the United States was established in Illinois in 1899. The juvenile justice system was founded on the principle of rehabilitation, with a focus on the offender, not the offense. In the 1950s and 1960s, many experts began to question the ability of the juvenile court to effectively rehabilitate delinquent youth; by the 1980s, the pendulum began to swing away from this rehabilitative approach toward more severe sanctions for juvenile offenders. By the 1990s, this turnabout was completed as authorities more strongly enforced the legal standards of juvenile crime.

The Arrestee Drug Abuse Monitoring (ADAM) program collects data from juvenile and adult arrestees across the country. Data were collected from more than 2,000 juvenile male arrestees in nine sites, and more than 400 juvenile female arrestees in eight sites. Usually half or more of juvenile arrestees tested positive for at least one drug. Juvenile arrestees interviewed by ADAM ranged from ages 12 to 18. In 2000, the largest proportion was between ages 15 and 17. Among those who tested positive for use of any drug, the largest group was age 17. In half of the sites, 70 percent of the juvenile detainees said they were still in school, ranging from 55 percent in Phoenix, Arizona, to 93 percent in San Antonio, Texas.[49]

THE DEBATE ON INCARCERATING DRUG ABUSERS

In 1982, the movement to send drug users to jail accelerated nationwide during the Reagan Administration's "War on Drugs." In state after state, penalties have become ever more severe in the last 25 years.

As of 2005, America imprisoned 2.1 million people, a record number that appears to keep rising each year. In 1985, the national incarceration rate was 313 per 100,000; in 2005, it was 715 per 100,000. The United States imprisons more people than does all of Europe, despite the fact that Europe has 100 million *more* people.[10]

According to the President's 2007 National Drug Control Strategy, education is a key component of preventing drug use and abuse, and thereby reducing demand for methamphetamine. However, between 1985 and 2000, states spent six times more money for prisons than for schools.[10]

The driving force behind the increase in incarceration may be the stricter penalties for drug offenders. But does it work? Eighty percent of people in prison have a drug problem, and many states are reexamining their policies, distinguishing between two questions: Is this a meth addict who has become a criminal to support his or her addiction? Or, is this a criminal with a drug addiction?[10, 51]

The Drug Court Program provides alternatives to incarceration for low-level offenders such as drug addicts. It uses the corrective power of the court to alter drug behavior, with a goal of abstinence and a healthy return to society. It costs about $35,000 a year to imprison a meth addict, and it costs about $18,000 to send that person to a drug treatment program. Drug Court uses a combination of escalating sanctions, mandatory drug testing, treatment, and strong aftercare programs.[10, 51]

Many states believe in this program's effectiveness. Minnesota has approved a measure that will shave off half of an inmate's sentence after completing a drug treatment program. Kansas mandates an 18-month drug treatment program for some offenders. Re-arrest rates for people that have gone through the drug courts are much lower (16 percent) than those who have not gone through drug treatment programs (about 55 percent).[51, 12]

Methamphetamine affects all aspects of a user's life—physical, mental, and social. The initial euphoria it produces is quickly replaced with depression and ruin. There is nothing magical about meth, aside from the speed with which it steals a person's health, alienates his or her family and friends, and thrusts users on a downward spiral. Personal experiences shared in this book attest to this drug's destructiveness. And while statistics show that teen meth use has declined slightly over the past few years, many teenagers still suffer from meth dependency and addiction. Stricter federal and state penalties for meth use, possession, manufacture, or distribution, coupled with tighter regulation of prescriptions and more specifically targeted treatment programs have helped curb meth's reach. Still, the ultimate responsibility for abstinence rests with each individual. Staying informed about the effects of drugs such as methamphetamine has never been easier. With numerous organizations, school educational programs, and Web sites debunking the myths of methamphetamine, people are better equipped to face life's challenges and make healthy decisions.

Glossary

acupuncture—A method, originally from China, of treating disorders by inserting needles into the skin at points where the flow of energy (Chi) is thought to be blocked.

anhedonia—The inability to feel pleasure.

anorexia—A persistent lack of appetite; an eating disorder where a person is in extreme fear of becoming overweight and excessively diets to the point of ill-health and sometimes death.

biorhythms—The body's natural cycles, such as sleeping and waking.

bronchodilator—A drug often used in the treatment of asthma that eases breathing by widening and relaxing the air passages to the lungs.

carcinogen—A substance that can cause cancer.

clandestine—Secret or furtive, and usually illegal.

cognitive behavior therapy—Therapy that focuses on how individuals think about what they feel or do.

electrolyte—An important ion in cells and blood, such as sodium and potassium.

euphoria—A feeling of great joy, excitement, or well-being.

extracted—To obtain something from a source, usually by separating it out from other material.

flammable—Readily capable of catching fire.

formication—A strong sensation of bugs crawling beneath the skin.

group therapy—A form of treatment in which patients, under the supervision of a counselor or psychologist, discuss their problems with a group of people who are also undergoing treatment.

half-life—The amount of time it take for half the amount of a drug or substance to be metabolized by the body.

HIV—Human immunodeficiency virus; a retrovirus that destroys the immune system's helper T cells; HIV is the virus that causes AIDS.

hyperthermia—An increase in body temperature to dangerous levels that sometimes causes convulsions or even death.

incarcerated—Imprisoned.

interventions—An action undertaken to prevent something undesirable from happening.

intoxicating—Capable of making someone drunk or stupefied with drugs.

intravenously—Occurring inside a vein.

ketosis—The overproduction of ketone bodies as a result of not eating for long periods of time; causes bad breath.

libido—Sex drive.

narcolepsy—A condition characterized by frequent, brief, and uncontrollable bouts of deep sleep, sometimes accompanied by an inability to move.

potency—The strength of a drug.

potent—Very strong or powerful.

precursors—Substances that, in nature, might be inactive, but when combined with another chemical, create a new product.

psychosis—A psychiatric disorder such as schizophrenia that is marked by delusions, hallucinations, incoherence, and distorted perceptions of reality.

quotas—A maximum quantity that is permitted or needed.

railing—Snorting crystalline meth powder.

renal—Having to do with the kidneys.

rush—A sudden and powerful onset of an emotion; a sudden feeling of elation and pleasure.

schizophrenia—A psychosis marked by delusional behavior and intellectual deterioration.

sober—Abstinence (complete restraint) from the use of drugs or alcohol.

stimulant—Something that increases bodily activity or acts like a stimulus.

synthetic—Made entirely from human-made chemicals; opposite of natural.

toxic—Poisonous; something that can cause serious harm or death.

volatile—Prone to sudden change; apt to become suddenly violent or dangerous.

xerostomia—An abnormal lack of saliva in the mouth.

Notes

1. Booth, S., A. Desimone, M. Hainer, and S. Wilson. "The Faces of Meth," *Teen People* 9, 2 (March 1, 2006): 114.

2. Gahlinger, Paul M., M.D. *Illegal Drugs.* New York: Penguin Group, 2004.

3. Narconon of Southern California, Inc. "Slang Terms for Meth." Available online. URL: http://www.stopmethaddiction.com/meth-slang.htm. Updated on June 29, 2006.

4. The Stonewall Project. "Weights and Measurements of Meth." Available online. URL: http://www.tweaker.org. Downloaded July 2006.

5. Narconon of Southern California, Inc. "The History of Meth." Available online. URL: http://www.stopmethaddiction.com/history-of-meth.htm. Updated on June 29, 2006.

6. Kuhn, Cynthia, Scott Swartzwelder, and Wilkie Wilson. *Buzzed.* New York: W.W. Norton & Company, Inc., 1998.

7. National Institute on Drug Abuse (NIDA). "Research Report Series—Methamphetamine Abuse and Addiction." Available online. URL: http://www.drugabuse.gov/ResearchReports/methamph/methamph3.html#short. Updated on February 4, 2005.

8. National Institute on Drug Abuse (NIDA). "NIDA InfoFacts: Methamphetamine." Available online. URL: http://www.drugabuse.gov/Infofacts/methamphetamine.html. Updated on June 3, 2005.

9. Keltner, Norman L., and David G. Folks. *Psychotropic Drugs.* St. Louis: Elsevier, Inc., 2005.

10. Johnson, Dirk. *Meth: America's Home-Cooked Menace.* Center City, Minn.: Hazelden, 2005.

11. WGBH Educational Foundation and Oregon Public Broadcasting. "Frontline: The Meth Epidemic." Available online. URL: http://www.pbs.org/wgbh/pages/frontline/meth/. Updated on March 21, 2006.

12. Office of National Drug Control Policy. "Interim Report: Interagency Working Group on Synthetic Drugs-2005." Available online. URL: http://www.whitehousedrugpolicy.gov/publications. Downloaded August 2006.

13. U.S. Department of Justice, National Drug Intelligence Center. "Crystal Methamphetamine Fast Facts." Available online. URL: http://www.usdoj.gov/ndic/pubs5/5049/5049p.pdf. Posted June 2003.

14. U.S. Drug Enforcement Administration (DEA). "Got Meth?" Available online. URL: http://www.justthinktwice.com/gotmeth/home.html. Downloaded on August 14, 2006.

15. U.S. Drug Enforcement Administration (DEA). "Map of DEA Meth Lab Seizures." Available online. URL: http://www.usdoj.gov/dea/concern/map_lab_seizures.html. Downloaded on August 14, 2006.

16. Weil, Andrew, M.D., and Winifred Rosen. *From Chocolate to Morphine.* New York: Houghton Mifflin Company, 1998.

17. Volkow, N.D., J.S. Fowler, G-J Wang, and J.M. Swanson. "Dopamine in Drug Abuse

and Addiction: Results from Imaging Studies and Treatment Implications." *Molecular Psychiatry* 9, 6 (June 2004): 557–569.

18. Substance Abuse and Mental Health Services Administration, Office of Applied Studies. "Drug Abuse Warning Network, 2004: National Estimates of Drug-Related Emergency Department Visits." DAWN Series D-28, DHHS Publication No. (SMA) 06-4143, Rockville, Md., 2006.

19. Johnston, L. D., P. M. O'Malley, J. G. Bachman & J.E. Schulenberg . "Monitoring the Future: National Survey Results on Drug Use, 1975–2005: Volume I, Secondary School Students." NIH Publication No. 06-5883. Bethesda, Md.: National Institute on Drug Abuse, 2006.

20. Schucker, D. "Nazi Labs." Available online. URL: http://www.okienarc.org/nazilab.htm. Downloaded on August 16, 2006.

21. Short, K. "Red Phosphorus Methamphetamine Labs." Available online. URL: http://www.okienarc.org/RedPlabs.htm. Downloaded on August 16, 2006.

22. Bianchi, Robert P., Manoj N. Shah, David H. Rogers, and Thomas J. Mrazik. "Laboratory Analysis of the Conversion of Pseudoephedrine to Methamphetamine From Over-the-Counter Products." Available online. URL: http://www.usdoj.gov/dea/programs. Downloaded on August 16, 2006.

23. U.S. Drug Enforcement Administration (DEA). "DEA Drug Seizures." Available online. URL: www.usdoj.gov/dea. Downloaded on August 14, 2006.

24. Midwest High Intensity Drug Trafficking Area (Midwest HIDTA), Iowa Governor's Office of Drug Control Policy. "Life or Meth: What's the Cost? Education Program." Available online. URL: http://www.lifeormeth.org. Downloaded on August 15, 2006.

25. Community Epidemiology Work Group. "Epidemiologic Trends in Drug Abuse: Advance Report, January, 2006." NIH Publication No. 06-5878. Bethesda, Md.: National Institute on Drug Abuse, 2006.

26. Community Epidemiology Work Group. "Epidemiologic Trends in Drug Abuse: Advance Report, Highlights, Executive Summary – Abuse of Stimulants and Other Drugs." NIH Publication No. 05-5280. Bethesda, Md.: National Institute on Drug Abuse, 2005.

27. Dupont, Robert L., M.D. *The Selfish Brain.* Center City, Minn.: Hazelden, 1997.

28. Jacobs, Andrew. "Battling H.I.V. Where Sex Meets Crystal Meth." *The New York Times.* February 21, 2006.

29. Nordahl, Thomas E., M.D. "Brain Region Recovery Possible In Former Methamphetamine Users." *Archives of General Psychiatry* 62 (2005): 444-452. Available online. URL: http://www.sciencedaily.com. Posted on April 22, 2005.

30. Blakeslee, Sandra. "This is Your Brain on Meth: A 'Forest Fire' of Damage." *The New York*

Notes

Times. July 20, 2004. Available online: URL: http://www. loni.ucla.edu/~thompson/ MEDIA/METH/nytMETH.htm. Downloaded June 2006.

31. Greater Dallas Council on Alcohol & Drug Abuse. "Methamphetamine." Available online. URL: http://www.gdca-da.org/statistics/meth/meth2. htm. Downloaded on April 22, 2007.

32. Sato, M., C.C. Chen, K. Akiyama, and S. Otsuki. "Acute Exacerbation of Paranoid Psychotic State After Long-term Abstinence in Patients with Previous Methamphetamine Psychosis," *Biological Psychiatry* 4 (April 18, 1983): 429–440.

33. The National Association of Counties. "The Criminal Effect of Meth onCommuni-ties." Political/Congressional Transcript Wire. July 5, 2005.

34. Johnston, L. D., P. M. O'Malley, J. G. Bachman, and J.E. Schulenberg. "Monitoring the Future: National Results on Adolescent Drug Use: Overview of Key Findings, 2005." NIH Publication No. 06-5882. Bethesda, Md.: National Institute on Drug Abuse, 2006.

35. Substance Abuse and Mental Health Services Administration, Office of Applied Studies. Wright, D., and N. Sathe. "State Estimates of Substance Use from the 2003–2004 National Surveys on Drug Use and Health." DHHS Publication No. SMA 06-4142, NSDUH Series H-29, Rockville, Md., 2006.

36. Manisses Communications Group, Inc. "Athletes Targeting Healthy Exercise and Nutrition Alternatives," *Alcoholism & Drug Abuse Weekly* 16, 47 (December 13, 2004): 6.

37. Goode, Erich. *Drugs in American Society.* 4th ed. New York: McGraw-Hill, Inc., 1993.

38. The National Center on Addiction and Substance Abuse at Columbia University (CASA). "National Survey of American Attitudes on Substance Abuse XI: Teens and Parents." New York: 2006.

39. The National Center on Addiction and Substance Abuse at Columbia University (CASA). "National Survey of American Attitudes on Substance Abuse VI: Teens." New York: 2001.

40. Substance Abuse and Mental Health Services Administration, Office of Applied Studies. "Treatment Episode Data Set (TEDS). Highlights–2004. National Admissions to Substance Abuse Treatment Services." DASIS Series: S-31, DHHS Publication No. (SMA) 06-4140, Rockville, Md., 2006.

41. Library of Congress. "Senate Report 109-293 (FY 2007 HIDTA and other pro-grams)." Available online. URL: http://thomas.loc.gov. Downloaded on August 28, 2006.

42. Zimmer, L., and J.P. Morgan. *Marijuana Myths, Marijuana Facts: A Review of the Scientific Evidence.* The Lindesmith Center, 1997.

43. UCLA Integrated Substance Abuse Programs: Methamphetamine. Available online. URL: http://www.meth-

amphetamine.org/html/treat-ment.html. Downloaded on April 24, 2007.

44. National Association of State Alcohol and Drug Abuse Directors. "2005 Fact Sheet: Methamphetamine." Available online. URL: http://www.nasdad.org/resource.php?doc_id=315. Downloaded on April 24, 2007.

45. Iowa Consortium for Substance Abuse Research and Evaluation. "Iowa Project: Year Six Report (September 2004)." Available online. URL: http://www.idph.state.ia.us/bh/common/pdf/substance_abuse/sa_oms_report.pdf. Downloaded on April 24, 2007.

46. University of California-Los Angeles (UCLA). "First Human Tests Of Antidepressant Bupropion As Methamphetamine Addiction Treatment Hold Promise." Available online. URL: http://www.sciencedaily.com. Posted on November 29, 2005.

47. Marshall, Lisa. "Alternative Clinics Offer Holistic Ways to Beat Addiction." *Alternative Medicine* (July/August 2006): 65–70.

48. National Institute on Drug Abuse (NIDA). "Mind Over Matter: Methamphetamine." Available online. URL: http://teens.drugabuse.gov/mom/mom_meth1.asp. Updated on June 14, 2006.

49. National Institute of Justice. "2000 Annual Report on Drug Use Among Adult and Juvenile Arrestees, Arrestees Drug Abuse Monitoring Program (ADAM)." NCJ 193013, April 2003. Also available online. URL: http://www.ojp.usdoj.gov/nij/adam/welcome.html. Downloaded on August 14, 2006.

50. Office of National Drug Control Policy. "National Drug Control Strategy." Available online. URL: http://www.white-housedrugpolicy.gov/publications. Downloaded August 2006.

51. Political/Congressional Transcript Wire. "U.S. representative Mark Souder (R-IN) holds a hearing on programs to treat victims of methamphetamine addiction." 2006 *Congressional Quarterly*. June 29, 2006.

52. *Genetic Engineering News.* "BioMarket Trends," Available online. URL: http://www.genengnews.com/articles/chitem.aspx?aid=1820&chid=0. Posted on August 1, 2006.

53. State Department of the United States, Bureau for International Narcotics and Law Enforcement Affairs. "2006 International Narcotics Control Strategy Report." Available online. URL: http://www.state.gov/p/inl/rls/nrcrpt/2006/. Downloaded August 2006.

54. U.S. Drug Enforcement Administration (DEA). "Federal Trafficking Penalties." Available online. URL: http://www.dea.gov. Downloaded on August 14, 2006.

Web Sites

CyberSober – Our Place
http://www.cybersober.com
> Our Place is an online prevention, education, and support resource for teenagers and their parents. The site offers times and locations, including maps, for adolescent 12-Step meetings and online teen meetings, as well as a teen chat and teen news.

DanceSafe
http://www.dancesafe.org

FRONTLINE: The Meth Epidemic
http://www.pbs.org/wgbh/pages/frontline/meth/
> From PBS, a 2005 investigation into the meth epidemic from all angles: social, medical, legal, trends. Includes live footage, interviews, and colorful graphs.

Meth Resources
http://www.methresources.gov
> A comprehensive, one-stop shop that offers up-to-date information on methamphetamine, and resources for communities, students, businesses, activists, etc.

The Montana Meth Project
http://www.montanameth.org
> A nationally recognized, high-impact advertising campaign that graphically communicates the risks of meth use. It's for teens, by teens. Includes personal stories, facts about meth, and gritty photos.

National Clearinghouse for Alcohol and Drug Information (NCADI)
http://www.samhsa.gov
> 1-800-729-6686
> Provides printed and online information about types of drugs and substance abuse. Toll-free number also provides referrals and information about treatment options.

Narcotics Anonymous
http://www.na.org/index.htm

National Institute on Drug Abuse (NIDA)
http://www.nida.nih.gov

Sobriety High
http://www.sobrietyweb.org/index.htm

The Oregonian Investigative Report:
"Unnecessary Epidemic: A Five-Part Series"
http://www.oregonlive.com/special/oregonian/meth/

A 2005 newspaper series that co-hosted the Frontline report. Features investigative journalism on meth and how it affects the community, the individual, and the country.

The Substance Abuse and Mental Health Services Administration (SAMHSA)
http://www.samhsa.gov
1-800-662-HELP

Call this hotline for help locating treatment resources quickly.

US Drug Enforcement Administration (DEA)
http://www.justthinktwice.com

An engaging and interactive Web site directed at teens. A section of the site is dedicated to meth, and includes graphic before-and-after pictures of meth addicts.

Further Reading

Braswell, Sterling R. *American Meth: A History of the Methamphetamine Epidemic in America.* Lincoln, Neb.: iUniverse, Inc., 2005.

Moore, Patrick. *Tweaked—A Crystal Meth Memoir.* London: Kensington Books, 2006.

Wilshire, Bruce. *Wild Hunger—The Primal Roots of Modern Addiction.* Maryland: Rowman & Littlefield Publishers, Inc., 1999.

Index

Index

About the Author

Randi Mehling is the author of six young-adult nonfiction books. A health communications specialist for 17 years, Randi holds a Master's of Public Health degree and has written on a wide variety of science and health topics. She is a published poet and essayist, and lives with her wonderful husband in New Mexico where they hike and backpack to their heart's delight.

About the Editor

David J. Triggle is a university professor and a distinguished professor in the School of Pharmacy and Pharmaceutical Sciences at the State University of New York at Buffalo. He studied in the United Kingdom and earned his B.Sc. degree in chemistry from the University of Southampton and a Ph.D. in chemistry at the University of Hull. Following post-doctoral work at the University of Ottawa in Canada and the University of London in the United Kingdom, he assumed a position at the School of Pharmacy at Buffalo. He served as chairman of the department of biochemical pharmacology from 1971 to 1985, and as dean of the School of Pharmacy from 1985 to 1995. From 1995 to 2001, he served as the dean of the graduate school and as the university provost from 2000 to 2001. He is the author of several books dealing with the chemical pharmacology of the autonomic nervous system and drug-receptor interactions, some 400 scientific publications, and has delivered more than 1,000 lectures worldwide on his research.